The First Session
with Seniors

Forrest Scogin

The First Session with Seniors

A Step-by-Step Guide

Jossey-Bass Publishers
San Francisco

Jossey-Bass books and products are available through most bookstores. To contact Jossey-Bass directly, call (888) 378-2537, fax to (800) 605-2665, or visit our website at www.josseybass.com.
Substantial discounts on bulk quantities of Jossey-Bass books are available to corporations, professional associations, and other organizations. For details and discount information, contact the special sales department at Jossey-Bass.

Manufactured in the United States of America on Lyons Falls Turin Book. This paper is acid-free and 100 percent totally chlorine-free.

Library of Congress Cataloging-in-Publication Data

Scogin, Forrest Ray.
  The first session with seniors : a step-by-step guide / Forrest
Scogin. — 1st ed.
    p.   cm.
  Includes bibliographical references (p.) and index.
  ISBN 0-7879-4743-1 (alk. paper)
  1. Psychotherapy for the aged.   I. Title.
RC480.54 .S365 2000
618.97'68914—dc21   99-6679

FIRST EDITION
HB Printing   10 9 8 7 6 5 4 3 2 1

Contents

To my family: Melanie, Allen, and Margo
And to my parents, who have given me so much

Foreword

Much has changed over the thirty years that I have been a clinician, supervisor, teacher, and student of psychotherapy. Therapy is briefer, more people have access to help, psychotropic medications are more effective, and the stigma associated with psychological help has decreased.

One issue, however, remains constant: therapists have always known that the first session is crucial for both emergency intervention and beginning the process of change. Current mental health practice, moreover, renders the first session even more preeminent, since managed care and insurance benefits are limited and the nature of treatment has focused more on problem solving and short-term goals. In fact, 40 percent of all psychotherapy clients today attend only a single session, and the rest typically have four or five meetings.[1]

As therapists we know that we must use the first session to

- Establish a relationship and working alliance

- Assess the need for crisis intervention

   Evaluate presenting problems and establish a diagnosis

   Explore emotions

Focus the problem(s)

Reach mutual agreement on what needs to be done

- Explore options for solution (one of the alternatives may be to continue therapy)[2]

Consequently, the First-Session Series has been launched with full appreciation for the magnitude of accomplishing these goals in a single session. Likewise, this series is also intended to demonstrate sensitivity and respect for the diversity of background, culture, and experience of clients we hope to serve.

Much can be said for the generic skills necessary for a successful first session, but most therapists are aware of the necessity of customizing our interventions to the specific needs of our clients. What we need to know for a successful first session with a teenager may be very different from what we need to know for a septuagenarian. Consequently, this series provides students, educators, and practitioners with essential knowledge of how to enrich existing therapeutic skill with specific information fine-tuned to meet the demands of diverse populations.

With these goals in mind, we asked Forrest Scogin to tell us how to increase the clinical efficiency of a first session with older adults. With sensitivity and proficiency, he opens the door by alerting us to the "demographic imperative" of this ever-increasing population. His experience comes alive as he walks us through the most common presenting problems and the hidden issues that may be their ultimate cause. He tells us what to expect, what to look for, how to manage a crisis, and—most important—how to establish the rapport necessary to accomplish these goals. He provides the comprehensive knowledge necessary to manage hearing, visual, cognitive, and physical limitations during a first session, and he also addresses such special issues as coordinating care with primary care physicians, dealing with loss and depression, overcoming special transference and countertransference issues, and more.

Discovering how basic therapeutic skills must be adapted to meet the needs of older clients is likely to inspire therapists to learn more about enhancing the effectiveness of their first sessions with other populations they serve. Upcoming titles in this series will provide the culturally competent direction necessary to facilitate first sessions with other groups that also require special sensitivity, including African Americans, adolescents, and substance abusers. With each new book in this series, we hope to instill not only greater understanding of your clients as a special group but also more compassion for the unique qualities of each individual. Finally, we hope that the wisdom, experience, techniques, and strategies our authors present will enhance the overall effectiveness of each first session.

August 1999   Jeanne Albronda Heaton
Athens, Ohio

Notes

1. Klienke, C. L. *Common Principles of Psychotherapy*. Pacific Grove, Calif.: Brooks/Cole, 1994, p. 176.

2. Heaton, J. A. *Building Basic Therapeutic Skills*. San Francisco, Jossey-Bass: 1998, p. 69.

Acknowledgments

I feel as if I'm at the Oscars . . . there are so many people to thank.

First, a big thanks to my wife, Margo, who put up with me while I worked crazy hours. She also helped me come up with more case material when my well had run dry. I also want to thank my kids, Allen and Melanie, for putting up with less time to kick the ball and read a story.

Graduate students with whom I have worked over the years have also taught me a lot about psychotherapy with older adults (probably more than they realize) while I supervised them. To the older adult clients with whom I have had the privilege to work: What can I say? I owe this book to you.

I can't forget my mentors in psychotherapy and aging: Martha Storandt, Larry Beutler, and Sol Garfield. Though this means I'll probably get more of the same good-natured ribbing, I want to thank my colleagues at the University of Alabama in the department of psychology. Their recurring question—"Are you done with the first twenty minutes of the first session yet?"—provided some appreciated comic relief.

Finally, I want to thank Jeanne Albronda Heaton, who kept me on task and provided useful feedback on my drafts. Thanks also for the Foreword.

The First Session
with Seniors

Introduction

Many clinicians view a first session with an older adult with the same enthusiasm they hold for their own prospect of becoming a senior. Decline, depression, despair—death. Who wants to deal with this?

If that were all there is to working with older adults, I too would find a new interest. Certainly, older adults experience decline and depression, but this is not all that happens. In contrast, I find this work intriguing. There is opportunity to discover

- The twists and turns of sixty-plus years of living fully

- The poignancy of watching someone overcome a life-long difficulty

- Ways to maintain hope in the face of illness and loss

- The wisdom that comes with finding integrity and meaning

These moments highlight my therapeutic career. They are why I maintain that working with older adults is so rewarding.

This affinity is captured by a phrase a senior colleague often shared with me: "You've got to be tough to be old." I'm often reminded of this as I listen to clients tell me of their physical ailments and the compensations they must make. But don't get me wrong. Older clients can present clinicians with the same frustrations in therapeutic work as any other group. For example, they resist treatment through entrenched tendencies, and they can be intemperately loquacious. Further, the complication of cognitive impairment lurks in the background and in many cases is ever-present. Nonetheless, I find that work with older adults has more high moments than low ones; I think you'll get the same assessment from my "gero" colleagues.

There are several reasons why I think a book on the first session with seniors is important for therapists. One is the demographic imperative—the absolute number and percentage of older persons in our country is rapidly rising. More and more clients will be older, particularly as postwar baby boomers reach later adulthood. It also appears to be the case that people born after World War II are evidencing more psychological difficulties. Thus, not only will there be more older adults in the future but there is every reason to believe they will be in need of greater behavioral health care than present older adults are.

Second, relatively few clinicians have received training in geropsychology. Whether you're a specialist or not, you surely already have older adults in your caseload. This creates a need for some guidance on how best to craft the most important session of psychotherapy: the first session. To do your best work, an understanding of the strengths and limitations of older clients is critical. For example, I have found older clients extremely conscientious in terms of keeping appointments, following through on homework assignments, and respecting therapist-client boundaries. On the other hand, cognitive and sensory declines make it unwise to use a "normal" pace of therapy.

Additionally, as treatments become shorter in terms of number of sessions, the importance of the first session is magnified. It may be the case that you will have only a few more sessions—or maybe just this one. A leisurely beginning to treatment is ill-advised since you might have only a few more sessions during which to reach treatment goals. Creating a maximally effective first session is good for everyone. The client obviously benefits. But so does the therapist, both personally and fiscally. The personal benefit comes from experiencing a sense of intimacy with the client that comes from sharing in his or her improvement. In addition, most clinicians working with older adults know that society benefits if human suffering and overall health care expenditures are reduced.

The final reason I think a book on the first session with elders is important is that the practice of psychotherapy has to be one of the most cognitively and emotionally complex of all activities undertaken by human beings. Breaking down the complex activities that take place, and then presenting them in more detailed fashion, is what teaching and learning are about. My goal is to make the details accessible for your critical appraisal and adaptation as it suits you.

The goals for this book are reflected in the chapters. It is my belief that optimal work with any group requires mastery of some basic information about the population. In the first chapter, I give readers a primer on the psychology of aging. We all continue to develop throughout our life span; however, since most therapists are younger than their older clients, they can't use their own experiences as a guide. We shall discuss the basic psychological, biological, and sociological issues older adults contend with that are relevant to first-session work.

In Chapter Two, we look at the typical presenting problems of older adults seeking psychotherapy. We talk about the routes by which older adults come to a first session of psychotherapy. Particular attention is paid to treatment initiated or facilitated by family members and the risks and rewards therein. The chapter gives an overview of the age-specific nuances of such presenting problems as depression, anxiety, substance abuse, sleep, and loneliness. We also look at age-specific problems of memory complaints and dealing with adult children.

Next come the action chapters. Chapter Three is about assessment and diagnosis. Work with older adults requires much greater attention to issues of cognitive and medical status. Because the two statuses are so important in work with older adults, the first session becomes a critical point of assessment. I review some informal and formal measures of cognitive functioning and offer some suggestions as to the circumstances under which one might conduct formal assessment. Very few older adults participating in psychotherapy have no health problems, or concomitant treatments that are unrelated to the presenting problem. I share some examples and highlight the bearing these may have on the process and outcome of psychotherapy. The direction, and even the feasibility, of treatment can be determined in large part during session one.

The second part of Chapter Three is on what I see as the good and the bad of diagnosis. Diagnosis is a necessary part of modern mental health care, though at times it approximates a square peg in a round hole. Insurers require the square peg to reimburse behavioral health care providers, so like it or not this is a reality. Conversely, diagnosis can provide clients and therapists with a convenient method of communication. The chapter includes discussion of some ideas about communicating these contrasting notions to older clients.

Chapter Four is devoted to what I consider the most important element in psychotherapy: the alliance. I present some ways to facilitate a working alliance with older adults. Demonstrating respect is one essential element in this process, as is demonstrating competence and understanding of issues that often affect older adults. A particularly sensitive area in the first session can be managing loquaciousness. For some older adults, age-related changes in the ability to inhibit interfering stimuli produce a rambling, stream-of-consciousness presentation that can make a first session difficult. Tactful management of this issue is important for immediate and long-term alliance building. The chapter ends with discussion of transference (son or daughter?) and countertransference (parent or grandparent?) reactions that have the potential to occur in a first session with an older adult.

In Chapter Five, on interviewing strategies for a first session, I begin to tie together all the aforementioned information with a step-by-step guide. The relation of cognitive status and interviewing process is discussed, as is the need to compensate for working-memory deficits shown by many older adults. I also give consideration to structured versus nondirective interviewing strategies. Involving family members in the initial session is revisited in this chapter.

Chapter Six covers crisis intervention necessitated by information obtained during the first session. This might arise from indications that your client should not be operating a motor vehicle, is in need of more extensive assistance with activities of daily living, or is suicidal.

Chapter Seven is a presentation of some thoughts on treatment planning and the value of using empirically supported treatment approaches. I present the maturity-specific-challenge model of psychotherapy, developed for work with older clients. I have found this model to be helpful when I consider a treatment plan for clients.

The book closes with case studies developing the major points made in the previous chapters. These cases present composites of clients I have worked with or who were seen by trainees under my supervision.

Throughout this book I focus on providing psychotherapy on an outpatient basis to community-dwelling older adults. Much of this material may also apply to work in long-term care settings, but my experiences have been predominantly in outpatient work.

I'm both a clinical scientist and a practitioner. My work with older adults is informed by research findings, and I argue vigorously for the relevance of integrating clinical research with clinical practice. I see this book as a conduit through which relevant research findings, and my clinical experiences, can be presented to readers who deliver service. Older adults deserve the best of what both science and practice can deliver.

Primer on the Psychology of Aging

Come grow old with me
the best is yet to be
Robert Browning

Older adults are different from younger adults in some obvious and some not-so-obvious ways. Physical differences are apparent (wrinkled skin and graying hair), whereas subtle differences may be revealed in attitudes and values elders tend to hold. In this chapter, I concentrate on several areas that are important for you to know as you enter a first session with an older client:

- The demographics of aging

- Diversity in aging

- Health

- Personality

- Perceptions of mental health

- Perceptions of mental health treatment

- Cognition and aging

- Sexuality and aging

- Sensory change

- Late-life development

As our populace ages, therapists need to possess some gerontological expertise. To conduct an optimal first session with older adults, therapists must have knowledge of aging in general but also of the older adults that make up a specific cohort. I find it fascinating to learn about the life experiences and the events known to the group of older adults who were there. Knowledge of these socializing events can help you relate more empathically to clients who present with very different histories from those of therapists who grew up and were trained in the years after World War II.

THE DEMOGRAPHICS OF AGING

We are an aging society. The absolute number and relative proportion of older adults are both increasing. Furthermore, persons eighty-five years of age and older are the fastest-growing age group in our population. How remarkable this is, when not too long ago living into old age was a relatively rare event. Just how dramatic this change has been is illustrated in Figure 1.1.

Among the reasons for the dramatic increase in longevity are improvements in public health and advances in medical care. There is even reason to believe that in the decades to come life expectancy (how long the average person can expect to live) and life span (the biological limits of longevity) will coincide, that is, many people will live to the biological limits of 110–120 years. This is known as the "rectangularization" of the survival curve. Figure 1.2 shows this trend in graphic form.

It is noteworthy that the male and female survivorship curves are not identical. This is the well-known difference in life expectancy as a function of sex. Women begin to outlive men in early adulthood, and by age seventy-five about 61 percent of the population is

Figure 1.1. Population of Americans Aged Sixty-Five and Over, 1900–2030 (Projected)

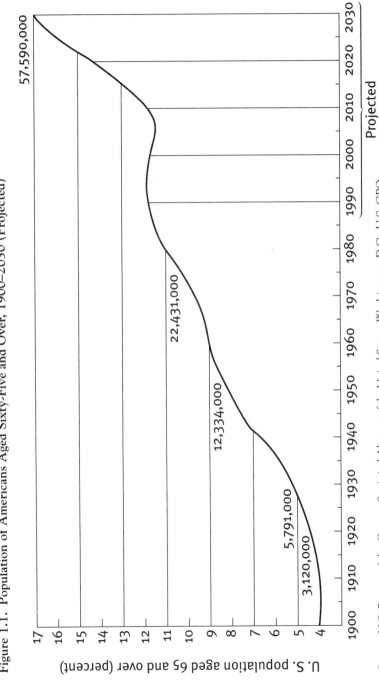

Source: U.S. Bureau of the Census. *Statistical Abstract of the United States.* Washington, D.C.: U.S. GPO. From J. Cavanaugh, *Adult Development and Aging* (2nd ed.). Copyright © 1993 by Brooks/Cole. Reprinted with permission of Global Rights Group.

Figure 1.2. The Rectangularization of the Human Life Span

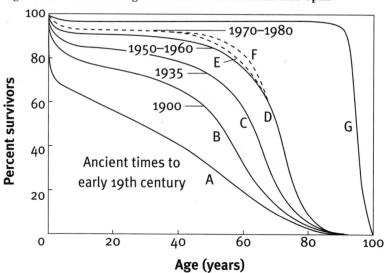

Key to curves

A–D	Male or female survivorship
E	Male survivorship
F	Female survivorship
G	Hypothetical idealized survivorship

Reasons for changes in the curves

A–B	Improved housing, sanitation, antiseptics
B–C	Public health, hygiene, immunization
C–D	Antibiotics, improved medical practice, nutrition, health education
D–F	Recent biomedical breakthroughs

Source: J. M. Rybash, P. A. Roodin, and W. J. Hoyer. *Adult Development and Aging* (3rd ed.). Copyright © 1995 by Brown and Benchmark. Reproduced with permission of The McGraw-Hill Companies.

Note: This graph shows human survivorship trends from ancient times to the present. These idealized curves illustrate the rapid approach to the rectangular survivorship curve that has occurred during the last 180 years.

female. At eighty-five, 70 percent of the population is female.[1] Figure 1.3 gives you a graphic image of this trend. What this means is that most of your older clients will be female. I estimate that about 75 percent of all my older clients have been female.

Many people assume that most older adults live in institutional settings such as nursing homes. Actually, only about 5 percent of those over sixty-five reside in institutions—to many people, a surprisingly low number. However, the rate of institutionalization is age-related in that approximately 25 percent of those eighty-five and older live in institutions.[2] This tells us a couple of things. First, growing old does not invariably (nor even most of the time) lead to the nursing home. Second, it means there are many older adults in the

Figure 1.3. Proportion of Men in Population by Age

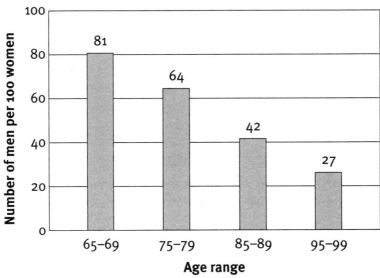

Source: U.S. Bureau of the Census. *Marital Status and Living Arrangements: March 1991.* Washington, D.C.: U.S. GPO, 1992. From D. E. Papalia, C. J. Camp, R. D. Feldman, *Adult Development and Aging.* Copyright © 1996 by McGraw-Hill. Reprinted with permission of The McGraw-Hill Companies.

Note: as the population ages, the proportion of men for every 100 women declines. One result is that older women are more likely than older men to live alone and to need help from their families and from society.

community who are possible consumers of outpatient behavioral health care—and there are more on the way. Finally, many nursing homes and retirement facilities employ mental health consultants.

Another common misconception is that most older adults live alone. Actually, this applies to only about 30 percent of community-dwelling elders; not surprisingly, the percentage is higher for women (41 percent) than it is for men (16 percent). This can be important background information to consider as you evaluate the nature of your clients' social support networks.

The absolute number and proportion of older adults in the United States will reach a crescendo in the near future; this is of particular relevance to those of us providing behavioral health services. The maturation of the baby boom, the large group of persons born soon after World War II, has been and will continue to be a notable cultural phenomenon. The leading edge of this group is now fifty years of age or older; in the next five decades, the baby boom will present significant challenges to behavioral health care.

For example, we know that depression is a recurrent disorder. Will this pattern of recurrence continue into old age for boomers, a group that is currently demonstrating far greater rates of depression (than earlier generations) already in their younger years? It seems safe to say that as the greying of America takes place, clinicians will increasingly see older adults as psychotherapy clients. This presents an opportunity for those who are ready.

DIVERSITY IN AGING

It probably goes without saying that "the elderly" are not all alike, but I'll say it anyway. One useful means by which to recognize this heterogeneity is to think in terms of the "young-old" (sixty-five to seventy-five years), the "old-old" (seventy-five to eighty-five years), and the "oldest-old" (eighty-five years and older). The notion of a typical "senior citizen" is a myth; after all, we are talking about a span of twenty-five to thirty years in the grouping we refer to as older adults. In a normative sense, a sixty-five-year-old is quite different from a ninety-year-old.

These differences manifest themselves in broad domains such as health status and cognitive functioning, but also in more subtle ways, such as values, lifestyle choices, and expectations that arise from sociocultural influences predominating at a given time. It's also true that a ninety-year-old may be more physically and cognitively fit than a sixty-five-year-old. In fact, gerontologists consider *chronological age* only one marker of "age."[3] It is also useful to think in terms of *biological age*, that is, a measure of the vitality of major organ systems. Another take on this issue is *psychological age*, the person's ability to engage in thinking, reasoning, memory, and other higher cortical processes that serve to adapt to demands of the environment. *Functional age* refers to the capacity for successfully completing advanced and basic everyday tasks, such as meal preparation, financial management, and bathing. Finally, *social age* suggest the roles that we play, such as father, retiree, or athlete. Persons who are not in sync with predominant role expectations for their chronological age group are noticeable; an eighty-two-year-old driving a high-powered sports car draws our attention and engenders speculation.

Age is thus a multidimensional construct. It helps me to think about my clients across the various dimensions of age, creating, if you will, an age profile. Think about a couple of older adults you know of similar chronological age; I predict they have different profiles. For example, I think of a seventy-eight-year-old woman with whom I worked. She was very active and fit, having a sixtyish biological age. Her psychological age was close to her chronological age in that she evinced age-consistent memory changes such as difficulty in free recall. Her functional age was that of, let's say, people in their fifties, in that she had no trouble with basic and advanced activities of daily living, other than those requiring strain on the joints or upper-body strength. As for social age, I would say she was "younger." Indeed, most of her friends were in their twenties and thirties, and her values and lifestyle were more in accord with middle-aged people.

Some gerontologists suggest there is greater heterogeneity among older adults than any other age group because the influence of such factors as lifestyle (for instance, smoking) and chance (auto accidents) have a much greater opportunity to exert influence. Put differently, there is more variance in a group of seventy-year-olds than in a group of five-year-olds (though kindergarten teachers may beg to differ!).

It is also the case that we are a multicultural society. Thus an eighty-year-old, second-generation, Asian American female may have very different values, beliefs, and experiences than an eighty-year-old, fifth-generation, European American woman. Cultural, as well as age-related, sensitivity is a must for effective work with older adults. For example, it is not uncommon for grandparents to provide extensive parenting to their grandchildren, particularly among African American families.

All of this is to say that in general anything in this book about older adults is probably wrong for any specific senior. I apologize.

HEALTH

Health is an area that holds some surprises when you consider older adults. Most seniors have at least one chronic health condition, perhaps an orthopedic problem, hypertension, arthritis, or cataracts. I can remember seeing only a few older clients who had no such health problems; indeed, most have had multiple conditions. However, survey data suggest about 70 percent of community-dwelling elders describe their health as "excellent."[4] Consistent with the above, most older adults do not need help with everyday activities, though this too varies considerably from the young-old (about 10 percent do not need such help) to the oldest-old (about 50 percent).[5] The picture that emerges is of older adults tending to adapt to health problems without major limitations, well into advanced aging. Older clients teach you a lot about the consequences of chronic health conditions and, more important, about the compensatory processes they use to maintain independence. For example, I remember an older client with extremely poor vision who had designed magnifying solutions for television, reading, medications, and the like; they were positioned so that she could move about her house smoothly and always have magnification at hand. A smart woman!

PERSONALITY

Does personality change over the life span? This question has stimulated what I can only describe as a staggering amount of research. I'm going to use the five-factor model of personality (aka the "big five") to guide this discussion because it has been applied extensively in gerontological research. The five factors are

1. Neuroticism
2. Extraversion
3. Openness to experience
4. Agreeableness
5. Conscientiousness

In brief, neuroticism is such things as anxiety, hostility, sensitivity to criticism, and guilt. Extraversion is characterized by assertiveness, sensation-seeking, and affability. Openness to experience can be described as willingness to try things out, being imaginative, and questioning the status quo. Conscientious people are dutiful, disciplined, and orderly. Finally, agreeable describes people who are trusting, modest, and straightforward. Costa and McCrae, using sophisticated methodology and thousands of volunteers ranging in age from young adulthood to the oldest-old, found remarkable stability across the adult years in these personality dimensions.[6] They concluded that between ages twenty-one and thirty personality appears to reach its final form. So, who you are now is who you are probably going to be, at least as far as the big five are concerned. Some have argued that assessing these broad traits may mask more subtle change. The rebuttal to this criticism has been that what seems like a change may in fact be due to a stable tendency, such as openness to experience.

Nonetheless, it seems plausible that some personality dimensions might change in later adulthood. An even more focused study of personality in more than three thousand older adults found little change over seven years.[7] Interestingly, these investigators did find differences such that present-day elders seem to be less rigid and less socially responsible than previous groups of older adults. Taken together, these results suggest that there is little change at the individual level (after you get through the tumultuous early-adulthood years) and that more difference is evident when you compare across generations.

As you work with an older adult, it is likely that you witness life-long patterns of personality functioning. Who she is is probably what she has been. Nevertheless, culture matters, because cohort or generational differences do exist. Today's seventy-year-old goes through a very different socialization experience from that of a seventy-year-old in 2015. For example, present elders were by-and-large born and raised in the years 1910–1940. An appreciation of historical events and the cultural zeitgeist from that period can inform clinical work with older adults. It is reasonable to assume this sensitivity should enable clinicians to perform more competently. Here are some examples of events and socializing influences:

- World War I
- World War II
- Stock market crash and the Great Depression
- Prohibition

- Segregation

- Shift from rural to urban society

For example, working with African American older clients (particularly in the South, where I live) reminds one of the effects of segregation. Stories of separate educational facilities, restrictions on the right to vote, and vigilante justice are painful reminders.

This is why it is so important to know something about history when you work with an older client. The person before you is a product in part of the sociocultural influences of his early adult years. It also means that you can't assume that change in personality is a result of aging. Clinicians must look to other causes to account for such changes if reported during a first session.

PERCEPTIONS OF MENTAL HEALTH

Differences exist in how people understand and experience mental health. Most striking are the differences seen across cultures. To take one example, the meaning, and antecedents, of suicidal behavior vary widely cross-culturally. Similarly, there are differences in the perception and expression of mental health among generations of Americans. There are several ways to illustrate this. One way to see generational differences is to examine epidemiological data on the prevalence of mental disorders. Some findings may surprise you. In the classic Epidemiological Catchment Area study, people sixty and over consistently reported lower rates of mental disorders than did any other age group.[8] Included were those disorders that I had been trained to believe were higher among elders, such as major depression. How could this be, given the losses and declines experienced by older adults?

There are a number of plausible explanations for this finding:

- Hardy persons who have survived to old age are less likely to manifest mental health problems.

- The reparative and supportive influences of church, school, and family have diminished in recent decades, such that younger groups experience more mental health problems.

- The rise of disinhibiting influences such as substance abuse and violence in media (films, television, and music) have contributed to greater expression of psychopathology in younger generations today.

- Older adults may attribute symptoms such as loss of energy or headaches to health problems when they are in fact symptoms of psychological distress.

Another explanation for the lower rates is what I have come to call "cohort stoicism." This is the stiff upper lip, the keep-it-to-myself style manifested by many of today's older adults. I have seen this on many occasions in psychotherapy clients and even more among older persons in the community. I remember working with an older man who had a list of health problems as long as your arm, was in constant pain, and was chronically fatigued. However, if you asked him how he was doing, he'd say "fine." Only if you pressed him would he admit "I'm not feeling well and nothing much interests me anymore."

The upshot of this is that older adults may underuse mental health services; specifically, they may underreport symptoms and concerns when they are involved in psychotherapy. Remember the discrepancy between chronic health conditions and self-rated health mentioned earlier? It's very consistent with this stoicism.

Sensitivity to this propensity is critical in the first session with an older adult. Seniors may minimize the degree of pain (physical and mental) they are experiencing. Developing a therapeutic alliance, beginning in the first session, facilitates an adaptive reduction of this stoicism. This topic is revisited in Chapter Two, on presenting problems, and Chapter Four, on the alliance.

PERCEPTIONS OF
MENTAL HEALTH TREATMENTS

Just as there are age differences in the prevalence and reporting of mental disorders, so are there differences in perceptions of mental health treatment. Many of today's elders were socialized at a time when mental health treatment was primarily for those with serious mental health problems. I observe remnants of this attitude in older patients I see. They often wonder if they are "crazy" when exhibiting only minor anxiety and depressive disorders. My perception is that this is a genuine question; seeking out or being referred for mental health treatment is prima facie evidence they are unable to fully manage on their own. Being unable to do so is a damning sign of weakness to many elders who are fiercely independent.

Seniors may also hold negative beliefs about psychotherapy. Such thoughts as *I'm too old to change or learn new ways* or *I've never talked about how I feel* or *My situation is hopeless and getting worse* may interfere with initiating or continuing treatment.

In my work, I spend time as needed in providing information about the prevalence of mental disorder, sharing anecdotes about people with similar experiences, and suggesting etiological formulations of their disorder. For example, imagine an eighty-seven-year-old client who had experienced a mild right-hemisphere stroke and then suddenly lost a sister to whom she was extremely close. I would tell this mildly depressed client that having depressive symptoms is the most common presenting problem for women her age, that I personally have worked with a number of people with similar symptoms, and that her problem was probably a result of her sister's death and her stroke. She's not crazy, and she's not weak. Sharing this information goes a long way toward maintaining dignity—a commodity in short supply for demoralized clients. When you meet for the first time with an older adult, the effort to help them see they are not aberrant or crazy and need not feel shame for seeking assistance with their problems is time well spent.

Elders may also tend to view psychotherapy as "just talk." Older adults may be used to the more directive and "prescriptive" approach of health care providers like physicians and optometrists. "How can just talking to someone help me?" they ask. My strategy, again, is to provide information on the effectiveness of psychotherapy. I also share with them the structure of treatment protocols that I use, in an effort to counter assumptions that psychosocial interventions are weak and meandering. For example, for clients having a primary diagnosis of general anxiety disorder, I present some of the findings that support the efficacy of geriatric anxiety treatment.[9] I also give a quick overview of a treatment approach I am probably going to use. My message is that we have stuff that works and we'll follow a plan, not just follow the seat of ole Doc Scogin's pants. I have found that older adults are quite receptive to this information (and this presentation).

COGNITION AND AGING

A primer on the psychology of aging as it relates to a first session of psychotherapy would be incomplete without discussion of cognitive change and stability in late adulthood. Cognition and memory have significant impacts on the process of psychotherapy and constitute one of the major differences in work with older clients.

Dementia

Almost all older adults experience some age-related changes in cognition. For some, the changes are the harbinger of progressive neurodegenerative disease, such as Alzheimer's. There are several types of dementia, including vascular dementia, diffuse Lewy body disease, and substance induced persisting dementia; Alzheimer's is the most prevalent form of dementia (50–65 percent). In its early stages, Alzheimer's disease (AD) is almost imperceptible from normal age-related changes. This is one of the reasons that older adults are so concerned when they experience memory lapses.

How are they (or anyone else for that matter) to know what this means? About 5 percent of those sixty-five years or older suffer from AD, with a sharp rise in incidence (from 15 to 50 percent, depending on the reporting source) for those eighty-five and older.

Thus, AD is clearly an age-related disorder. One of the reasons it has become such a topic of interest in the past thirty years is that only recently have large numbers of people been living long enough to develop the disorder. Those of you who have worked professionally with or cared for a person experiencing AD know that it is devastating. Beginning with loss of higher cortical functions such as reasoning and intelligence, the disease gradually impairs the ability to control bodily functions and eventually contributes to death. Worse, the devastation is spread out over eight to ten years in most cases.

As a clinician working with older adults, you are confronted with issues related to dementia. Here are some signs to look for to distinguish AD from normal aging:

- Getting lost in one's neighborhood (versus getting lost in new surroundings)

- Putting things in inappropriate places (unpaid bills in the sock drawer) versus simply misplacing things

- Inability to do oft-repeated meal preparation (versus a complex task such as preparing a new meal)

Warning signs such as these warrant formal assessment, a topic I broach in Chapter Two.

Age-Consistent Cognitive Changes

The majority of older clients you see for a first session in outpatient psychotherapy are experiencing cognitive changes consistent with growing older. These changes are typified in the statement "My memory is not what it used to be." They are probably right, and the changes have definite relevance for your first-session work. For example, you can provide reassurance to many clients by sharing information with them about the distinctions between age-consistent changes and dementia.

Normal age-related changes primarily occur in short-term or working memory. This diminution is apparent in those tasks requiring cognitive effort, such as recalling recently learned information (trying to remember what was on the news last night), paying attention to complex or divided activities (trying to remember what someone has just said to you while you're reading the newspaper), or responding speedily to a question or request.[10] Older adults perform almost all cognitive tasks slower than do younger adults.

On the other hand, some aspects of memory functioning, such as remote memory (the name of your best friend when you were growing up), memory of previously learned and well-rehearsed knowledge (how many feet in a yard?), and vocabulary (the definition of *serrated*) show little decline (or even increase) in late adulthood. These fund-of-knowledge activities have been called "crystalized intelligence" by some gerontologists.[11] When declines begin to occur in crystalized intelligence, suspicion of dementia arises.

Psychotherapy as typically practiced is a fast-paced, abstract, and attention-demanding activity. This is exactly where normal-functioning older adults have the most problems. Deemphasizing rapid recall of recently learned information, moving at a slower pace, and providing memory aids to assist learning and recall are suggested compensatory strategies. I develop this topic further in Chapter Five, on interviewing strategies.

It is also a good idea to know something about cognition and aging because you are probably asked by some of your older clients to help them improve their memory. Memory complaints are relatively frequent in the older clients I have seen. Not often the major complaint, but frequently a contributing factor. I remember supervising a case in which an older man had become almost agoraphobic as a result of his self-reported memory problems. He was concerned that he would get lost or forget his parking place.

Research has demonstrated that memory training can improve objective[12] and subjective[13] memory functioning among nondemented older adults.

Objective memory functioning concerns performance on laboratory or everyday memory tasks such as remembering names, recalling words from a list, or reminding yourself to take an umbrella on a cloudy day. Subjective memory functioning is how well you believe your functioning to be. For example, when I ask you how often your memory gives you a problem or how serious your memory lapses have been, I am assessing subjective memory functioning. Most memory-training programs involve instruction in mnemonic techniques, use of physical reminders, and relaxation training. Interestingly, the improvements seen through memory training are larger in objective memory functioning than in subjective memory functioning. During a first session, your ability to speak intelligently about the nature of and treatment for memory concerns can be a great boost to alliance building with an older client.

SENSORY CHANGES

Sensory deficits can interact with more purely cognitive deficits to present further challenges in a first session with a senior. Diminished hearing and vision functioning are age-related and in extreme cases can stymie the flow of interviewing. By age seventy-five, about three-fourths of the population experience some hearing difficulties.[14] Hearing loss for high-pitched sounds (presbycusis) is the greatest. I encountered an example of this recently. An older female participant in one of our depression studies requested a male interviewer because she had more trouble hearing women. My approach? I talk . . . real LOW . . . and real SLOW. Shouted inquiries do not promote shared empathy—or better hearing.

Visual difficulties are also a factor to consider in a first session. Depth-perception problems, increased sensitivity to glare, and reduced peripheral vision are among the visual processes observed to decline with age. There are several ramifications of these visual changes for a first session with a senior. First and fundamentally is getting the client to your office. Elders often express a preference to avoid sessions where they must drive in the dark. Midday sessions seem to work best, when traffic is less hectic and the light is stronger. But once you've got them there, a single-spaced, three-page client form set in a 10-point font won't cut it. If your forms or questionnaires are printed on glossy paper, it just compounds the problem.[15] Large (but not huge) print, on a nonglossy material, to be filled out in an area with good lighting all optimize conditions to compensate for visual difficulties.

Some of your older clients will also present with visual disease. I recall working with an older client who experienced *macular degeneration,* the loss of receptor cells in the central part of the retina that makes it difficult to distinguish fine details as needed for reading or watching television. Try focusing on something; now, what you see in your peripheral vision is akin to *all* they see. A blurry, unfocused visual field. My client was functionally blind because of this pathology (as are one out of five adults over age seventy-five).[16] She never saw me clearly, but she was able to make out some images if I sat to her side.

Cataracts and *glaucoma* are two other pathologies that can interfere with visual functioning and are relatively common among elders. Most older adults develop cataracts, opaque areas on the lens of the eye. The result is that less light passes though to the retina, causing blurred vision. Glaucoma, the build-up of fluid pressure in the eye, affects about 14 percent of those over eighty.[17] Both of these disorders compound the visual changes that are a normal part of aging. Clients with these diseases need even greater accommodation along the lines mentioned earlier. For example, touch may be used to convey empathy to a visually impaired elder, for whom your facial expression of concern and forward-leaning posture of interest may be lost.

Let me be clear, however: these sensory difficulties are simply challenges to be meet, not insurmountable obstacles to successful interviewing. Most of the suggestions I make are commonsensical if you know something about the changes that tend to occur among seniors. When these challenges are met and an alliance is established, it is extremely gratifying, not only because it is a privilege to work with older adults but also because it is so often deeply appreciated by clients who tend to be avoided because of these difficulties.

AGING AND SEXUALITY

Did you know that about 45 percent of those between seventy-one and seventy-five and about 55 percent of those between sixty-six and seventy report having had sex at least once in the preceding month? The same survey indicated that among those who were sexually active, the frequency of sex per month was about 4.5 for those sixty-six to seventy and 3.5 for those seventy-one to seventy-five.[18] When I present these data to young adult students, they are flabbergasted! I hope I've revised upward your expectations of sexuality in the senior years. As with so many things in life, people who are sexually active when younger are more likely to remain active when older.[19] The recent development of the medication sildenafil citrate (aka Viagra) has also changed the landscape of aging and sexuality. If early promise is sustained, medications of this sort may allow more men and women to be sexually active than ever before. So don't expect older adults to be sexually inactive.

Some changes in sexual function are age-related. For example, men have less-firm erections, they are not maintained as long, and the volume of ejaculation is decreased. For women, reduced levels of estrogen may produce less elasticity in the vaginal wall and less vaginal lubrication. However, intimacy may be expressed through other means: touching, physical closeness, and emotional sharing. Though it may be uncomfortable for some clients (and clinicians), discussion of sexuality and intimacy is no less important for older clients than for other populations. This is because sexual needs persist for older adults.

LATE-LIFE DEVELOPMENT

In concluding this primer, I want to touch on psychosocial developmental issues in late adulthood. I have often found it useful to conceptualize the presenting problems of my older clients within a developmental framework. A number of developmental theories have been posited that are relevant to older adults, including those of Levinson and Loevinger.[20] The most useful theory in my work has been that of Erikson.[21] As you probably know, Erikson's "eight stages of man" suggest that we move through challenges revolving around particular themes. As a reminder, here are the eight stages:

1. Trust versus mistrust
2. Autonomy versus shame and doubt
3. Initiative versus guilt
4. Industry versus inferiority
5. Identity versus identity confusion
6. Intimacy versus isolation
7. Generativity versus stagnation
8. Integrity versus despair

For example, in early adulthood the issue of intimacy is a predominant theme. A common misconception of Erikson's theory is that after one passes the age for which a stage is most relevant, one reaches resolution of the primary issue for that age (for example, intimacy). Instead, individuals concurrently deal with a variety of these issues at any given time. In other words, the stages are not "passed" but revisited across the life span. For example, difficulties with establishing mature intimacy earlier in life leave one vulnerable to isolation in late adulthood, not to mention despair.

The eighth stage of the life-span theory concerns the major psychosocial task of the older adult: ego integrity versus despair. This task is an ongoing challenge that becomes more poignant as the end of life approaches. In essence, the issue is to review one's life and determine if it has been worthwhile. This process, often called life review, involves reminiscence and sharing one's life history. Ego integrity is a movement toward acceptance of a life well lived. Here are Erikson's own eloquent words: "A meaningful old age, then, . . . serves the need for that integrated heritage which gives indispensable perspective on the life cycle. Strength here takes the form of that detached yet active concern with life bounded with death, which we call wisdom. . . . To whatever abyss ultimate concerns may lead individual men, man as a psychosocial creature will face, toward the end of his life, a new edition of the identity crisis which we may state in the words, 'I am what survives me.'"[22]

In my experience, it is often helpful to frame clients' problems (and triumphs) in terms of ego integrity versus despair. I recently worked with a retired electrician. This married, otherwise happy person suffered from lifelong social phobia. As he recounted the history of his problems during our first session, I began to feel the sense of lost opportunities he had suffered as a result of his disorder. A deeply spiritual man, he was regretful that he had avoided speaking up in his Sunday school classes and during church services for fear of embarrassment. He felt as if he had let himself (and God) down by not sharing his belief. This client was not in what I would call deep despair, but it was clear to me that he wanted to spend the remainder of his days being a role model to his children and grandchildren. I worked with him for several months on relaxation and cognitive coping strategies, and he experienced a remarkable degree of improvement, not only in terms of his disorder but also in his sense of integrity.

When you see a senior for a first session, you can expect to hear issues akin to this. Conceptualizing them within a developmental model can be helpful to you and your client. I've found this works particularly well for clients who are guilty about past behaviors (say, inadequate parenting) and realize there is nothing they can do to change events that have transpired. I treat and supervise predominantly depressed older adults. Quite often, the struggle these clients are going through to make amends with their past, in an effort to face the future with integrity, is almost palpable. Much can be done to change the meaning a person ascribes to the past. Psychotherapy, beginning with a productive first session, is one means to do so.

So Much to Say

There is so much more that could be discussed in a primer on the psychology of aging. You'll want to think about death and bereavement in your first-session work with elders. I have seen clients for whom loss of a spouse or an adult child has precipitated cascading decline similar to what follows a serious medical crisis, such as breaking a hip. During the first session, it's a good idea to ask about losses because some seniors may not have acknowledged to themselves the impact.

You also benefit in your work by knowing something about topics such as caregiving, retirement, . . . and wisdom (one of my favorites). How is wisdom relevant to a first session of psychotherapy (you wisely ask)? Because in the midst of declining physical abilities, losses, and the threat of dementia, wisdom is often in abundance. Smith and Baltes define wisdom as "exceptional insight into human development and life matters, exceptionally good judgment, advice, and commentary about difficult life problems."[23] In a clever study, older and younger adults did not differ too much when asked to provide counsel and perspective on a scenario affecting a young person, but the older adults were wiser when responding to a scenario involving an older person.[24] So many of my older clients have shared with me their wisdom that I feel rewarded. You will too.

In the Appendix of this book, I provide additional readings that are helpful for those desiring more background in geropsychology. In this primer I have drawn from textbooks written by geropsychology colleagues I want to acknowledge.[25] I firmly believe that solid knowledge of basic research with older adults is a great advantage for those who work with seniors.

———————

Gerontology is a burgeoning field of inquiry, with important new discoveries in medicine and behavioral sciences occurring frequently. If you plan to work with older adults, it behooves you to stay up-to-date. Looking at a good textbook (at the college senior level) or perusing some of the top journals can be a good start. Continuing education opportunities pertaining to psychotherapy with older adults are becoming more commonplace at conventions and conferences. Finally, let your clients teach you—they have experience!

The learning experience begins with referral and presentation of the presenting problem, the topics to which Chapter Two is devoted.

Notes

1. Rybash, J. M., Roodin, P. A., and Hoyer, W. J. *Adult Development and Aging.* (3rd ed.). Madison, Wis.: Brown and Benchmark, 1995.

2. American Association of Retired Persons (AARP). *A Profile of Older Americans.* Washington, D.C.: AARP, 1994.

3. Birren, J. E., and Birren, B. A. "The Concepts, Models, and History of the Psychology of Aging." In J. E. Birren and K. W. Schaie (eds.), Handbook of the Psychology of Aging. (3rd ed.). San Diego: Academic Press, 1990.

4. AARP (1994).

5. Bureau of the Census. *Sixty-Five Plus in America*. Washington, D.C.: U.S. Government Printing Office, 1995.

6. Costa, P.T., Jr., and McCrae, R. R. "Set Like Plaster? Evidence for the Stability of Adult Personality." In T. F. Heatherington and J. L. Weinberger (eds.), *Can Personality Change?* Washington, D.C.: American Psychological Association, 1994.

7. Schaie, K. W., and Willis, S. L. "Adult Personality and Psychomotor Performance: Cross-Sectional and Longitudinal Analysis." *Journal of Gerontology: Psychological Sciences*, 1991, 46, 275–284.

8. Robins, L. N., and others. Lifetime prevalence of specific psychiatric disorders in three sites. *Archives of General Psychiatry*, 1984, 41, 949–958.

9. Stanley, M. A., Beck, J. G., and Glassco, J. D. "Generalized Anxiety in Older Adults: Treatment with Cognitive Behavioral and Supportive Approaches. *Behavior Therapy*, 1997, 27, 565–581; Scogin, F., and others. "Progressive and Imaginal Relaxation Training for Elderly Persons with Subjective Anxiety." *Psychology and Aging*, 1992, 7, 418–424.

10. Papalia, D. E., Camp, C. J., and Feldman, R. D. *Adult Development and Aging*. New York: McGraw-Hill, 1996.

11. Horn, J. L. "The Theory of Fluid and Crystalized Intelligence in Relation to Concepts of Cognitive Psychology and Aging in Adulthood." In F. I. M. Craik and S. Trehub (eds.), *Aging and Cognitive Processes*, Vol. 8. New York: Plenum, 1982.

12. Verhaeghen, P., Marcoen, A., and Goossens, L. "Improving Memory Performance in the Aged Through Mnemonic Training: A Meta-Analytic Study." *Psychology and Aging*, 1992, 7, 242–251.

13. Floyd, M., and Scogin, F. "Effects of Memory Training on the Subjective Memory Functioning and Mental Health of Older Adults: A Meta-Analysis." *Psychology and Aging*, 1997, 12, 150–161.

14. Fozard, J. L. "Vision and Hearing in Aging." In J. E. Birren and K. W. Schaie (eds.), *Handbook of the Psychology of Aging*. (3rd ed.). San Diego: Academic Press, 1990.

15. Akutsu, H., Legge, G. E., Ross, J. A., and Schuebel, K. J. "Psychophysics of Reading: Effects of Age-Related Changes in Vision." *Journal of Gerontology: Psychological Sciences*, 1991, 46, 325–331.

16. Papalia, Camp, and Feldman (1996).

17. "The Aging Eye." *Harvard Women's Health Watch*, Dec. 1994, pp. 4–5.

18. Marsiglio, W., and Donnelly, D. "Sexual Relations in Later Life: A National Survey of Married Persons." *Journal of Gerontology: Social Sciences*, 1991, 46, 338–344.

19. Masters, W. H., and Johnson, V. E. *Human Sexual Response*. Boston: Little, Brown, 1966.

20. Levinson, D. *The Seasons of a Man's Life*. New York: Knopf, 1978; Loevinger, J. *Ego Development*. San Francisco: Jossey Bass, 1976.

21. Erikson, E. H. *Childhood and Society*. New York: Norton, 1950.

22. Erikson, E. H. *Identity: Youth and Crisis*. New York: Norton, 1968, pp. 140–141.

23. Smith, J., and Baltes, P. B. "Wisdom-Related Knowledge: Age/Cohort Differences in Response to Life Planning Problems." *Developmental Psychology*, 1990, 26, 494–505.

24. Staudinger, U. M., Smith, J., and Baltes, P. B. "Wisdom-Related Knowledge in a Life Review Task: Age Differences and the Role of Professional Specialization." *Psychology and Aging*, 1992, 7, 271–281.

25. Cavanaugh, J. *Adult Development and Aging*. (2nd ed.). Pacific Grove, Calif.: Brooks/Cole, 1993; Rybash, Roodin, and Hoyer (1995); Papalia, Camp, and Feldman (1996).

2

Referrals and Presenting Problems

The first session of psychotherapy with a senior usually includes a presentation of problems much like what one would hear from a younger client. But don't be deceived. Depression, anxiety, and relationship difficulties tend to be salient concerns, but beyond these categorical labels the similarities end. In this chapter I discuss some of the differences that exist among such relatively common presenting problems as depression, anxiety, and substance abuse. Following that, I talk about some of the problems you may hear only during an initial session with an older adult. To begin the chapter, let's consider some of the ways in which seniors are referred for outpatient psychotherapy.

"WHAT BRINGS YOU TO THE CLINIC TODAY?"

One of the sage pieces of advice I received while in training was that if you ask the client "What brings you to the clinic today?" and the response is "A car," you got trouble. This is apocryphal of course, but it amuses me. In actuality, what brings older adults (like anyone else) to psychotherapy is referral. So let's discuss the referral process.

As an independent private practitioner, I have received referrals from a variety of sources, including adult children of older clients, primary care physicians, psychiatrists, psychologists and social workers without expertise in aging, administrators of senior-citizen facilities, spouses, and last but not least the seniors themselves. In this chapter, I want to focus on referrals from adult children, physicians, other mental health professionals, and administrators because these pose some interesting challenges.

The Adult Child Referral

Involving family members in the treatment of an older adult is the norm rather than the exception. On many occasions, the family member primarily involved is an adult child. I've had referrals arranged from children living thousands of miles away who have very little contact with their parent. The treatment contact is often initiated or facilitated by a son or daughter who assumes some degree of caregiving. Sometimes the referral leads to family therapy, in which parent, adult child, and others are involved; but usually the referral is pursuant to individual therapy for the older adult.

How to handle the involvement of family members can also be a bit ticklish. For example, a daughter who makes the initial contact with her mother's physician, who then refers the case to me, may quite legitimately want to participate in the first session with her depressed mother. The daughter calls and schedules the appointment and arrives with her somewhat frail mother. What do I do? For an initial session, my inclination is to include family members if assent is given by the older adult; but I make it clear that some of the session will be spent without family members present. In most cases, family members (adult children included) are understanding and willing to leave the therapy to therapist and parent after the first session.

The problems identified by adult children include perceptions that mom or dad seems sad, worried, disinterested, or somehow affectively changed. Other problems identified by adult children tend to revolve around cognitive issues, such as forgetfulness or the ability to drive or handle finances. The underlying question seems to be, "Is my mother becoming demented?" or "Does she need more assistance?" Implicit in these questions are concerns about the changing nature of the relationship of parent to adult child (and, more personally, "How in the heck are we going to deal with this?"). As you work through the referral process and the initial session, the relationship dynamics of adult child and older parent are revealed.

Here are two examples of topics from which relationship issues may emerge during the initial session. Therapists need to evaluate the extent of consensus on what the problems are.

- An adult child says, "My dad is sad and not interested in the things he used to enjoy, like visiting with his friends and working in the yard." But Dad says "I'm just tired, and I'm eighty-two; that's not a mental illness, is it?"

- A mom says, "I'm having a little trouble handling my finances," but her adult son says, "She's headed for financial disaster."

Actually, empirical research has some light to shine on estimates of impairment. Research indicates that significant others tend to report more problems with activities in daily living than the older adults themselves do. Whose appraisal is more accurate in any given case is based on clinical judgment and dispassionate structured assessment.

The interpersonal history of the family becomes most sensitive when the problem presented by the adult child is something to the effect of "My father has become difficult to handle and I need you to fix him (or tell me what to do)." The trick in such cases is to achieve a state that one of my mentors, Larry Beutler, advocated to me: "Be of service to all and a servant of none." Because working with older clients, particularly at the point of referral and in the first session, involves working with family members, being caught in the midst of decade-long family issues can be perilous.

Here's an example from my work. An eighty-three-year-old retired Italian American retired high school principal was referred to me by his primary care physician for treatment of anxiety. My client also had several chronic medical conditions, among them diabetes and respiratory difficulties. His daughter set up the appointment, provided transportation, and at her father's insistence participated in the initial session. It was clear that the relationship between daughter and father had been strained for decades. But his declining health prompted a rapprochement. My client's daughter said, "His anxiety has gotten to the point that he is scared to take a walk in the backyard or do much of anything except watch TV." My client said, "My nerves are bothering me, but I'll be OK."

Now, throw in my client's wife, who was angry at her daughter ("Our daughter has given us fits since she was fifteen") and a son who lived a thousand miles away who was convinced he knew it all, and you've got dynamics galore. The son (by his sister's account) was critical of his family and said if he were there "things would be taken care of." Of course, he was rarely there to do anything. After careful evaluation during the first session, it turned out that the father did need some assistance but didn't want to burden his daughter. To further the bind, his wife wasn't able to handle his palpable anxiety. I asked my client, "What do you want?" and was surprised by the eloquence with which he elucidated his goal: "To enjoy what time I have remaining."

This example illustrates a situation in which the parent-child relationship interferes with solving the problem at hand. Conversely, there are situations in which the senior and the adult child have a supportive and productive relationship that can be enormously beneficial to the outcome of the first session as well as any treatment thereafter. On several occasions, I have worked with older clients who agreed to an initial consultation only with the encouragement and cajoling of their offspring. For seniors without a spouse, an adult child may be the only source of collateral information that is available. Further, adult children facilitate treatment by, for example, encouraging compliance with homework assignments or generally urging continuation when progress is slow.

All in all, my experiences working with referrals from adult children have been positive. However, it is interesting and challenging to work with a family member who is similar in age to me, while doing psychotherapy with a client who is somewhat like my parents—but more on countertransference later!

Physician Referrals

The majority of my referrals come from primary care physicians who know that I am a clinical geropsychologist. If you begin to accept referrals of older adults from primary care physicians, there are a few things to keep in mind. First, make sure everyone's expectations are realistic. Patients may be persuaded to come to you because of your specialty and interests, and they may expect results that you cannot deliver.

I remember a seventy-four-year-old European American man referred to me who had been treated with a variety of psychoactive medications for confusion, anxiety, and his tendency to be overly dependent. Nothing seemed to help much, but the physician thought that behavior therapy would have the greatest likelihood of success. It didn't, and the family was disappointed—in fact, a bit angry with me. If I had it to do over again, I would spend more time during the first session working with the family on their goals for treatment. I would also spend more time in communication with the physician, educating him to the prognosis so he could relay it to the family.

Another area that is important in working with physician referrals is to know something about psychopharmacology. Older clients are typically on one or more medications; if your referral is from a physician, you can jump the certainty factor up to about 100 percent. You want to know something about the major psychoactive medications, such as antidepressants and anxiolytics, but also about how these and other medications interact.[1] Ask the physician(s) or a knowledgeable nonphysician if you don't know about something you learned during the first session. For example, I treated a man who could not take an antidepressant because of a life-threatening cardiovascular disease, despite being quite depressed. After our first session, I asked his referring physician why this was the case and received a thorough explanation. I think the physician and my new client were happy that I had done so.

Another reason you need to be up to speed on the common psychoactive compounds is that you will periodically be asked for an opinion (just an opinion) on what medication might be best suited for a particular client. The diagnostic impressions you gather during a first session can help you in this endeavor. For example, are there indications of several anxiety symptoms in the depressive disorder? This may indicate the choice of a particular antidepressant.

Here's a situation that comes up regularly. What do you do when you are informed that a client has been referred to you but the client doesn't call? I usually phone the staff member who initially called me and give her times when I am available. I ask her to call the patient and schedule the appointment. Many older adults are reluctant to speak to mental health professionals, and having the primary care doctor or staff person make the appointment is usually a solution whenever a referral call is not forthcoming.

Another situation that commonly arises is that the referred patient calls and you or your staff are unsure the senior can comprehend—or even hear—what you are telling them. I always encourage a client to get out pencil and paper, write it down, read it back to me, and then place it in a prominent location. If the client indicates he cannot write, I ask him for the number of someone who can help get the information written down. This is usually an informal caregiver, a spouse, or a neighbor. If the whole process seems marred by lack of communication (either through hearing or cognitive impairment), I turn the arrangements over to the referral source.

My collaborative work with primary care physicians has for the most part been a pleasure. Working with older adult clients is frequently a multidisciplinary undertaking, with the primary care physician as the treatment coordinator. The ability to work within this framework is important to the opportunity to work with (and more important, I believe, succeed in treating) elders.

Other Mental Health Professionals

I sometimes receive referrals of older adults from other clinicians. One of my colleagues who was seeing a family with a child diagnosed with an attention-deficit, hyperactivity disorder (ADHD) became aware of problems being experienced by the live-in grandmother. This was a wonderful chance for collaboration among clinicians working with individuals across the life span. Other clinicians may refer if you begin to establish a reputation for work with older clients. This has happened to me in complex cases, such as mildly demented or paranoid seniors.

Psychiatrists are also a source of referral. Those who are biologically oriented may eschew psychosocial interventions while still seeing adjunctive value in psychotherapy. I have found geriatric psychiatrists to be quite good referral sources, perhaps because they are likely to keep up with the literature on the psychosocial treatment of mental health issues in older adults.

A final source of referrals is administrators or staff members of facilities that serve seniors: assisted-living facilities, activity centers, and governmental agencies. These referrals tend to be infused with a spirit of advocacy. Unlike the somewhat dispassionate referral from a physician or other clinician, these referrals come with negotiations about place, time, and fees. In other words (rightly, I believe), these individuals are working as a surrogate family member. Your attitude toward pro bono work and whether you are willing to see clients outside of your office may be tested by referrals from these sources.

Now let's talk about some of the distinguishing characteristics of the presenting complaints you may get from older adult clients.

PRESENTING PROBLEMS WITH A TWIST

The presenting problems of older adults are more alike than different from those offered by other age groups. But it's the dissimilarity I focus on in this section.

Depression

Let's start with depression since it's a major presenting problem for older adults. One of the major differences in the presentation of geriatric depression is in somatic symptoms. Fatigability, difficulties in concentration and memory, sleep disturbances, changes in sexual interest, and so on can be difficult, if not impossible, to disentangle from normal age-related changes, physical illnesses, or neurodegenerative disorders such as Alzheimer's disease.

In many of the cases I have seen or supervised, these age-related changes and physical illnesses are coexistent, creating an especially complex etiological and diagnostic picture. For example, we recently conducted depression assessments for patients at a rehabilitation hospital. These older adults were recovering from major orthopedic surgeries such as hip and knee replacements. A few days after surgery, they were assessed for depression. I believe you can imagine the difficulty in determining if symptoms were part of a depressive syndrome or otherwise. For instance, a patient complaining of sleep difficulties may do so for any of several reasons: pain, being in a strange environment, or the result of a medication effect. Don't forget, however, that they may also have sleep difficulties because of depression.

In evaluating these tough cases, knowing something about age-related changes in sleep helps. Whereas in younger adults difficulties in onset and maintenance of sleep are of diagnostic significance, with older adults sleep disturbance is a much less reliable indicator of depression. Furthermore, the nature of the sleep complaint tends to vary by age. The sleep complaints of seniors are more often about sleep maintenance rather than problems with sleep onset. Sleep, and other highly sensitive indicants of depression, can become quite complicated when reported by an older adult. So, what can you do? Be knowledgeable about age-related changes in somatic indicants of depression, ask lots of questions about the temporal relation of the symptoms to other nonsomatic symptoms (sadness, guilt, tearfulness), and make sure you rule out medical problems as a cause of the symptoms. Here are a couple of examples:

- "You say you've had pain problems for a long time. You also say you get tired easily. Do you think the tiredness is related to your pain? Or does it have more to do with your recent loss of interest in activities?"

- "You say you've had some trouble with waking up during the night for the past ten years or so. Has that gotten worse since you started feeling sad and guilty?"

It was the diagnostic quagmire created by symptoms such as diminished energy levels, concentration problems, and digestive difficulties that created the need for and subsequent development of a frequently used self-report depression inventory, the Geriatric Depression Scale.[2] The GDS contains no specific items on the somatic indicators of depression. Why, you might ask? The answer is that items of this kind, when completed by older adult respondents, did most poorly in detecting depression, as concurrently determined by diagnostic interviews conducted by geriatric mental health professionals.

The GDS has demonstrated good reliability and validity across a number of samples, including the mildly demented, nursing home populations, and community respondents. So the GDS is a good choice in screening for depressive disorders, particularly if time is of the essence.[3] The inventory comes in versions with thirty, fifteen, ten, and four items.[4] Here are the items from the GDS-4 that I use to screen for geriatric depression:

1. Are you basically satisfied with your life?
2. Do you feel that your life is empty?
3. Are you afraid that something bad is going to happen to you?
4. Do you feel happy most of the time?

It's important to consider that the difficulties already mentioned in accurately identifying depression are further complicated as the senior's degree of cognitive impairment worsens. Complicating factors are poorer recall of recent events, diminished ability to think abstractly, and difficulty in comprehending spoken or written language. The GDS surmounts these obstacles to some extent by having a simple yes-no response format. Response formats that include multiple-choice questions, such as the Beck Depression Inventory,[5] can be difficult for elders with working-memory limitations.

The bottom line is that diagnosis of a depressive spectrum disorder in an older adult requires careful consideration. Symptoms may not be what they appear to be and are often multiply determined. Use a good instrument such as the GDS, ask many questions, and learn about the changes associated with aging.

Anxiety

The picture with anxiety is somewhat different. The most frequently observed anxiety disorder among elders is generalized anxiety disorder (GAD), with relatively fewer cases of social phobia or panic disorder.[6] The age-specific nuance of GAD tends to be the "what" of the anxiety, that is, the content or focus of the worry. Not surprisingly, older adults are likely to worry about health, and younger age groups are likely to worry about family and finances.[7]

Concerns about something so realistic as health can lead us to miss the impairment, and consequently the suffering, caused by worry and anxiety. "It's no wonder she's worried about her health—she's frail" I have caught myself saying. I have worked with several older adults who indicated decades-long problems with anxiety that were dismissed by health care professionals as normal or not worthy of intervention. My point is not to fall prey to this tendency to minimize excessive worry and anxiety about understandable concerns (health, for instance).

The tendency to underpathologize also holds true for depression, where symptoms are sometimes viewed as simply part of getting older. Anxiety and depression are *not* natural consequences of growing old. These disorders can and should be vigorously treated.[8]

Substance Abuse

The twist on substance abuse with older adults is that illicit drug abuse is relatively rare, whereas abuse and misuse of prescription and over-the-counter medications is more likely.[9] Older adults use more medication than other age groups and with increased use comes risk of misuse. Some of the problems may be related to greater susceptibility to adverse reactions, and complicated dosing schedules required by multiple medications. In a related vein, older patients are also less likely to ask questions of their prescriber or pharmacist.[10] And of course seniors may abuse prescription drugs to ease the pain of depression, anxiety, or loneliness. A first-session interview with a senior should always include an inventory of prescribed and OTC medications presently being taken. The clinician should be alert to any symptoms that may suggest an adverse reaction to pharmacological treatment.

Alcohol abuse can be a hidden problem among older adults. Because they are often less involved in activities such as work or parenting, alcohol problems may go unnoticed. Alcohol abuse is categorized as early onset (those having abused alcohol prior to old age) or late onset (those abusing alcohol for the first time during old age). Late-onset cases are more linked to psychosocial stressors, such as the death of loved ones, health problems, or loneliness.[11]

Problem drinking may exacerbate age-related changes such as poorer memory functioning and shallower sleep. Drinking may also create difficulties with prescription and OTC medications. Older adults may be less likely to admit to alcohol use or abuse for fear of embarrassment. Many elders were socialized during a time in which alcohol use was prohibited or considered sinful. When I query about alcohol, I phrase the questions along the lines of "When you drink, how much do you typically drink?" or "If you drink, how much do you usually drink?" This takes a little burden off as far as admitting to a "bad" behavior.

Keep in mind that older adults show increased sensitivity to most psychoactive substances, including alcohol. Larger effects from smaller doses can lead to problems, such as drunkenness from the two drinks one used to enjoy during middle adulthood.

UNIQUE PRESENTING PROBLEMS

The preceding section discussed age-related differences in three common diagnostic syndromes. Depression, anxiety, and substance abuse are prevalent across the adult life span. I now discuss some presenting problems that tend to be unique among older adult clients:

- Resolving issues with adult children

- Caregiver depletion

- Memory complaints

- Grief, especially protracted grieving

- Compensating for functional limitations

- Death

Resolving Issues with Adult Children

In my outpatient psychotherapy with older adults, the most frequently presented issue is that of conflict with a spouse or adult children. I focus on the latter. Though I have already discussed the parent–adult-child relationship as it relates to referral, here it comes up again. It often emerges during a first session that a depression or anxiety disorder is related to one of life's most important activities: raising a child or children. An older adult's appraisal of someone's success as a parent is very often a basic theme in life review and a heavy determinant of ego integrity for the senior. Older adult clients may look back at their child rearing with regret, believing they did not show enough love, were not effective in setting limits, or were abusive.

This sense of regret or lack of closure may be fostered by the current behavior of the adult child. Adult children who themselves are having troubles (say, raising their own children or engaging in substance abuse) may provide vivid confirmation of the older adult's perceived shortcoming. This perception may be further reinforced by a poor current relationship with the adult child. All this is made more poignant by the senior's perception that time is limited in life and what was done cannot be changed.

In many cases, these perceptions are exaggerated and dysfunctional, and thus grist for the psychotherapy mill. Observing this anguish over parenting on repeated occasions has had such an impact on me that I now offer the following advice to anyone who (naïvely) thinks I might have something worthwhile to say about the key to happy old age: do right by your children. For those older clients who cannot say they have done right by their children, it is necessary to do a great deal of work in helping the senior understand his or her strengths and weaknesses as a parent. Quite often I find that my clients received very poor parenting themselves and were ill equipped to meet the challenge of raising children. This doesn't objectively change anything, but it can assist an older adult who is in despair cope better with the time remaining.

Caregiver Depletion

Another issue frequently presented by older clients is caregiver depletion. The caregiver client is often a spouse caring for a demented or frail mate. Caregiving is a hard job, both emotionally and physically. I do not hesitate to say that some of the most heroic stories I have ever heard involve family caregivers. Nonetheless, caregivers can become overloaded. Research indicates rather high rates of depression,[12] suppressed immunocompetence,[13] and other afflictions for those who provide care. Knowledge of the problem behaviors often exhibited by demented persons—such as wandering, repetitive questioning, and personality change—can be very useful in work with family caregivers.

Some caregiver referrals are for adult children who are themselves old and caring for a still-older parent. Issues that cut across three and even four generations are not uncommon. For example, I worked with an African American woman in her early sixties who was caregiving her older parents, while concurrently providing care to her grandchildren. She felt exhausted and more than a little used. Quite commonly, we encounter those (usually women) who are "in the middle." That is, they are caring for aging parents and their own children. Couples who have children later in life are more apt to be in the "sandwich generation."

Some good news is that research suggests psychosocial intervention can lead to diminished negative affect and depletion among caregivers.[14] A major focus in my work with caregivers has been in identifying and developing social support. Another focus has been in presenting caregivers with behavioral techniques that may help them manage care-recipient behaviors. For example, in a first session I would like to know whom a caregiver feels she can trust for advice, whom she can call on when help is needed, and if she receives negative social support (in the form of others who are critical of her efforts). Or, I might help develop routines that provide stability and security to memory-impaired older adults.

It's also good to know something about such local resources as caregiver support groups, respite care, and adult day care. I'm quick to share this information with clients during an initial session.

Memory Complaints

Difficulty with memory is another complaint that you may hear only from an older adult client. Such a complaint should prompt at least cursory, if not extensive, evaluation of cognitive functioning (to be covered in Chapter Three). If this evaluation results in a finding that the deficit is within nonpathological or age-consistent ranges, but the client is still concerned, then psychotherapy with a memory-training component is the treatment of choice. However, before delving into treatment, let's look further at the nature of memory complaints among older adults.

First, memory complaints are very frequent in older adults and even more frequent when anxiety or depression is present.[15] Put differently, a positive correlation between depression and extent of memory complaints is well established in the literature on clinical aging. Thus memory complaints, such as forgetting names and misplacing objects, can be exaggerated in the presence of affective distress. Interestingly, memory complaints tend to be less frequent as the degree of cognitive impairment becomes more pronounced. This paradox probably reflects lack of awareness evident in dementia patients.

I recommend that you ask this question during the first session with a senior: "How's your memory?" You'll get a few responses of "Fine," but more often you'll hear "Not what it used to be" or "Not good." I have some recommendations for further assessment in Chapter Three.

Grief

Another presenting problem is grief. Usually when we think of grief, it is following the death of a loved one. Older adults typically experience multiple losses of significant others. Imagine the devastation that follows the death of a spouse after fifty years of marriage. I remember working with a European American woman who experienced a profound depressive episode following the unexpected death of her husband. He had been the focus of her life, and he reciprocated by pampering her. My work with her was on maintenance of emotional well-being, following intensive inpatient treatment with ECT and pharmacotherapy. It was as if she needed to create a new identity, one that did not require him but honored his memory.

Another devastating loss is the senior who loses an adult child or grandchild. With older adults living longer, this "out of turn" event becomes an increasing possibility. People who are already vulnerable because of losses in physical and mental functioning may be overcome when such a tremendous psychosocial stressor occurs. Bereavement that becomes major depression—defined by the DSM-IV as symptoms two months after the loss—is found in a fair portion of the depressed older adults that we see in our depression studies.

We must also be aware of another type of grief: that experienced by an older adult as a loved one shows the inexorable decline of Alzheimer's disease. Alzheimer's is the most frequently occurring and well-known of the neurodegenerative disorders. As the brain dies from Alzheimer's, the sufferer slowly loses functional abilities. These losses are most pronounced in the areas that make us who we are: memory, intelligence, personality, and other higher cortical functions. As the disease progresses, sometimes over years, the person who was no longer exists. For many caregivers, this loss is experienced concurrently with the stress and burden of providing almost continuous assistance in the activities of daily living. It is a private loss, for the sufferer lives on; there is no funeral to provide closure, and the caregiver must carry on. Identification of these less-obvious grief reactions is a challenge for those beginning work with seniors.

Compensation

Issues that frequently arise in working with seniors are the compensations they must make for changes in health or functional ability. For example, one of the major decisions an older client or family member may be faced with is giving up the car keys. This may be the result of a stroke, declining vision, or difficulty in reacting quickly to complex stimuli. Similarly, engagement in socially rewarding activities such as religious services may be limited. In a first session, it is important to ask questions (fill in the blanks) along the lines of "Are you unable to do things because of _____ ?" and "What do you do to handle the problems with _____ ?" Some older adults are so fiercely independent that they are quite reluctant to ask for help. Others do not have the skills necessary to access resources. On the other hand, I have seen examples of compensation that are quite remarkable: people who have a well-orchestrated transportation system though they cannot drive, or people who have reminder telephone calls arranged so as not to forget daily events. One of your tasks as a therapist working with older adults is to aid in designing and implementing compensatory strategies. Assaying needs for and skills in compensation is proper fare for a first session.

Death

Work with older adults also includes providing services to those who are dying. You will usually be part of a palliative care group that includes physicians, nurses, and clergy. Hospice is probably the best known model of palliative care, in which the philosophy is to help the dying "live until they die." Therapists may provide supportive interventions in the hospital, in the client's home, or on an outpatient basis. I have found attention to the issue of ego integrity particularly important in working with dying patients. Facing death is no longer an abstraction. Most of the dying clients with whom I have worked were calm about death itself, but they wanted to take care of matters such as mending strained relationships or settling financial affairs. Some of this acceptance of the end of life has to do with timing. People in the old-old and oldest-old groupings know that death beckons, whereas middle-aged and young-old adults are more likely to feel impending death is untimely. As I discuss in Chapter Four, the potential for countertransference issues in work with dying patients is strong. Supportive consultation and supervision are always advisable.

Older adult clients come to psychotherapy with several presenting problems that are unique to them as a group. They may also come (or you may go to them) via referral paths that are somewhat different from those of other adult patients. Appreciation of these differences allows you to conduct a more efficient and accurate first-session assessment and diagnosis. Chapter Three is devoted to these activities.

Notes

1. Schneider, J. "Geriatric Psychopharmacology." In L. L. Carstensen, B. A. Edelstein, and L. Dornbrand (eds.), *The Practical Handbook of Clinical Gerontology*. Thousand Oaks, Calif.: Sage, 1996.

2. Yesavage, J. A., and others. "Development and Validity of a Geriatric Depression Screening Scale: A Preliminary Report." *Journal of Psychiatric Research*, 1983, *17*, 37–49.

3. Scogin, F., Rohen, N., and Bailey, E. "Geriatric Depression Scale." In M. Maruish (ed.), *Applications of Psychological Testing in Primary Care Settings*. Hillsdale, N.J.: Erlbaum (forthcoming).

4. D'Ath, P., and others. "Screening, Detection, and Management of Depression in Elderly Primary Care Attenders: The Acceptability and Performance of the 15 Item Geriatric Depression Scale (GDS15) and the Development of Short Versions." *Family Practice—An International Journal*, 1994, *11*, 260–266.

5. Beck, A. T., and others. "An Inventory for Measuring Depression." *Archives of General Psychiatry*, 1961, *4*, 561–571.

6. Scogin, F. "Anxiety in Old Age." In I. H. Nordhus, G. R. Vanden-Bos, S. Berg, P. Fromholt (eds.), *Clinical Geropsychology*. Washington, D.C.: American Psychological Association, 1998.

7. Person, D. C., and Borkovec, T. D. *Anxiety Disorders Among the Elderly: Patterns and Issues*. Paper presented at the 103rd annual convention of the American Psychological Association, New York, Aug. 1995.

8. Schneider, L. S., Reynolds, C. F., Lebowitz, B. D., and Friedhof, A. J. *Diagnosis and Treatment of Depression in Late Life: Results of the NIH Consensus Development Conference*. Washington, D.C.: American Psychiatric Press, 1992.

9. Dupree, L. W., and Schonfeld, L. "Substance Abuse." In M. Hersen and V. B. Van Hasselt (eds.), *Psychological Treatment of Older Adults: An Introductory Text*. New York: Plenum Press, 1996.

10. Olins, N. J. "Pharmacy Interventions." In S. R. Moore and T. W. Teal (eds.), *Geriatric Drug Use: Clinical and Social Perspectives*. New York: Pergamon Press, 1985.

11. Schonfeld, L., Dupree, L. W., and Rohrer, G. E. "Age-Related Differences Between Younger and Older Alcohol Abusers." *Journal of Clinical Geropsychology*, 1995, *1*, 219–227.

12. Gallagher, D., and others. "Prevalence of Depression in Family Caregivers." *Gerontologist*, 1989, *29*, 449–456.

13. Kiecolt-Glaser, J. K., and Glaser, R. "Caregiving, Mental Health, and Immune Function." In E. Light and B. Lebowitz (eds.), *Alzheimer's Disease Treatment and Family Stress: Directions for Research*. (DHHS publication no. ADM 89–1569). Washington, D.C.: U.S. Government Printing Office, 1989.

14. Gallagher-Thompson, D., and Steffen, A. M. "Comparative Effects of Cognitive-Behavioral and Brief Psychodynamic Psychotherapies for Depressed Family Caregivers." *Journal of Consulting and Clinical Psychology*, 1994, *62*, 543–549; Zarit, S. H. "Interventions with Family Caregivers." In S. H. Zarit and B. G. Knight (eds.), *A Guide*

to *Psychotherapy and Aging*. Washington, D.C.: American Psychological Association, 1996.

15. APA Working Group on the Older Adult. "What Practitioners Should Know About Working with Older Adults." *Professional Psychology: Research and Practice*, 1998, 29, 413–427.

3

Assessment and Diagnosis

In my opinion, the two main areas that distinguish work with seniors have to do with medical and cognitive status. Because assessment of these domains is often undertaken during the first session of treatment with an older adult, assessment of cognitive functioning and medical status is the focus of this chapter. I cover some of the circumstances in which formal evaluation is indicated and some useful tools for conducting brief screening.

I am not an advocate of routine psychological testing for clients entering psychotherapy. I take this position because I am not convinced that a satisfactory cost-benefit ratio is achieved; put more directly, I have seen no data suggesting that routine psychological evaluation produces superior outcomes. However, I am very much an advocate of using delimited, targeted psychometric evaluation when questions relevant to treatment arise. Questions about an older adult's cognitive functioning are certainly treatment-relevant.

ASSESSMENT OF COGNITIVE FUNCTIONING

In Chapter One, I presented some basic information on how cognitive functioning changes as we age. To reiterate, there is no doubt that many cognitive functions become less efficient with aging. The issue for the clinician conducting an initial session with an older adult is to gauge the degree of impairment (if any) and what changes in treatment (if any) are indicated.

With some referrals, the need for formal evaluation is evident. Let's take as an example a phone call I received recently from a daughter who wished to have her mother seen in our geropsychology clinic. She reported to the intake worker that "my mother is very forgetful, and whenever we discuss this with her she gets defensive and angry." The daughter went on to say, "Mother is having crying spells, which she has never had before, and she doesn't seem to want to do things like read or watch her soap operas." The daughter was concerned about her mother's safety (she lives alone), because she had left the stove on and water running on several occasions. In her words, "I'm afraid she's going to set the house on fire and burn up with it." Here are some thoughts on this case as they came to me following the telephone consultation.

First, there is no assurance that we will ever see this client (the mother) because she may refuse the appointment. I tell the daughter: "Your mother might not agree to come to the clinic. If you think it would help, I could talk to her about what we will be doing." Nonetheless, we begin to make plans for an initial session on the assumption she will show.

Cognitive evaluation is clearly called for, based on the shard of information we now have, but getting the mother to agree to it requires sensitivity. Confronting the mother right away with a formal evaluation tool that demonstrates her weaknesses is unwise. Instead, I think it better to ask some questions about cognitive functioning during the interview and proceed to a formal psychometric mental status screening if the mother is willing. For example, I ask the mother, "Tell me about some of the things that are hard for you to do around the house" and "Do you sometimes find yourself being forgetful?" I gauge further inquiry based on her openness to questions of this type. (In this case, she turned out to be fairly responsive to questions of various sorts, as in "Your daughter is concerned about you leaving the stove on and setting the house on fire. Are you concerned about this?" However, it was not until the second session that she permitted me to do a formal mental status evaluation.)

What to Look for

Suppose indications are that screening for cognitive impairment with psychometrically sound instruments is necessary. The first and most obvious question: Is cognitive impairment evident? It is easy to determine extreme cases on either end of a continuum of cognitive status. The older adult who speaks eloquently, follows the nuances of spoken communication, and has little difficulty with recalling recent information needs no evaluation of general cognitive functioning (or needs it only if a particular complaint about cognitive functioning is voiced).

For example, I remember a first session with a depressed Asian American woman in her sixties who was particularly concerned about a memory lapse she had experienced: she forgot the name of her deceased husband. Being depressed, she magnified and catastrophized this lapse into a sign of disrespect to her husband's memory.

She said, "I must be losing my mind if I can't remember his name." I asked her to stay a little longer for the first session and conducted a mental status exam (see the later section "Mental Status"). She performed at a level that indicated no impairment. I went one step further and gave her a name-and-face recall task that we use in memory training studies.[1] In this task, pictures of twelve persons are given names (for instance, "Mr. Gladney"). Following presentation of the names and faces, we show the faces again and the participant is asked to supply the name. I showed her that her score was very much like those of other nondemented persons her age.

Did this convince her she was all right? No. Her belief that she was losing her mind was overdetermined—that is, her depression, her relationship with her husband, her compensation for age-related memory changes, and many other factors were bound up in her belief. Nonetheless, in such instances objective information can be reassuring to clients who wonder if they are becoming demented.

It is important to remember that difficulties in cognitive functioning can be a result of something else, so avoid jumping to conclusions. Problems such as depression, a painstaking and ponderous style, or focal neurological impairment could mimic cognitive difficulties. Depression is known to produce cognitive slowing ("psychomotor retardation"), and it can even mimic dementia in extreme cases. A slow and thoughtful style can simulate cognitive impairment as an older adult very carefully thinks things out before responding. As with some of my professorial colleagues, if you ask them what time it is, they'll tell you how the clock works. A minor stroke, for example, may lead to difficulties in speech articulation (dysarthria) that cause one to believe a memory deficit is present.

The senior who presents with moderate to severe dementia probably does not need a brief assessment of cognitive function. Instead, he needs a referral to his physician for a neurological or neuropsychological consultation. Individuals of this sort have significant difficulty with receptive and expressive language, reveal poor recall of information, and are unable to perform some activities of daily living without assistance. For example, a retired engineer may have difficulty coming up with the words *steering wheel* and instead say "the thing you use to turn a car—it's round." This same, once highly competent individual may now need assistance in picking out clothes, since without supervision he is likely to put on multiple pairs of underwear. In-session observations of this kind plus the reports of significant others obviate the need for a formal mental-status examination.

Having eliminated the two ends of the cognitive continuum, we now have the more difficult in-betweeners. For these individuals, attunement to cognitive issues is important. Much information can be obtained through an initial assessment interview, with or without formal psychometric screening.

Probably the first question to ask a client is "What kind of memory difficulties do you experience?" Almost everyone (young and old) will say, "I have problem remembering names" or "I misplace things." When I ask for examples of these difficulties, they are quite often benign or well within expectations ("When I go to reunions for retired workers I can't remember the names of people I worked with for thirty years"). I usually ask them, "Did anyone else seem to be having this problem?" They confess the "problem" was epidemic! If I observe no other indications of cognitive impairment, then I am pretty certain memory functioning is within age expectations.

I also ask older clients how serious they feel these memory failures are (that is, whether they are easily dismissed annoyances or reason for concern). As I pose questions of this sort, I am assaying subjective cognitive functioning, which may not necessarily be isomorphic with objective cognitive functioning. Subjective memory functioning is how good you think your memory is, how much of a problem memory lapses are for you, and how much effort you make in compensating for your memory shortcomings. Objective memory functioning refers to performance on psychometrically sound measures of memory and cognition, such as list or paragraph recall tasks.

Generally, I find it better to start with interviewing about subjective memory functioning in cases where cognitive function is an issue. I base my interview on research conducted with older adults.[2] Two principal domains that I ask about are the number of memory problems the person experiences and the degree of seriousness she associates with these memory lapses.

For example, I might ask "How often do the following present a memory problem to you?" after which I enumerate names, appointments, phone numbers used frequently, things people tell the client, words, and losing the thread of thought in conversation. I also ask my client, "How much does it bother you when you have a memory failure?"

True to form, some folks can't remember what they can't remember; if so, I begin rattling off some situations: "Do you forget people's birthdays? Do you have problems remembering to do household chores?" I then follow with the seriousness question, to ascertain the distress associated with the memory lapses: "When you have problems with remembering things people tell you, how much does it bother you?" I have had clients with very few problems but who are quite concerned, and I've had clients with lots of problems (though not demented) who take it all in stride.

If I get some indication during the first session that my client has concerns about cognitive functioning or if in the absence of expressed concerns he appears to have cognitive difficulties, I may obtain permission to conduct a brief psychometric screening. In the latter circumstance, I might say: "Have you noticed that your memory is not what it used to be? Most folks notice changes as they get older. I'd like you to take a few minutes to do some things that would give us a better idea of the changes you've experienced. After we've finished we can talk about the results. OK?"

What are some signs of cognitive difficulty that would prompt a brief psychometric evaluation? You might find elders who

- Take a long time to respond to questions (response latency)

- Frequently lose their train of thought

- Have difficulty with relatively undemanding memory tasks

For example, we do not expect most seventy-year-olds to have trouble remembering the name of the town in which they were born. Nor when we ask them a relatively straightforward question (for example, "Did you have any trouble finding a parking place?") do we expect a five-second pause before the answer. A rambling, tangential style of speech also begins to raise concern.

One concrete sign of impairment is forgetting recently learned episodic information—for example, being unable to answer such questions as

- "Have you reported your concerns to your physician?"

- "When did you last talk to your oldest son?"

- "What's the name of the president?"

You know it is time to open the topic of psychometric assessment when self-report ("I don't remember as well as I used to"), subtle signs (response latency), and obvious signs (trouble remembering recent events) converge. In these cases, cognition could be a variable in the success of treatment.

Mental Status

Upon deciding that a formal assessment of cognitive functioning is desirable, a clinician must decide on a good instrument. Of the number of useful instruments for cognitive screening, here I discuss only one, the Mini-Mental State Examination (MMSE).[3] The MMSE is a standard in the field. This brief instrument is used in a variety of research and clinical settings and as such has developed a high communicability quotient, to wit, if I tell a "gero" colleague that a client scored an 18 on the MMSE, my colleague has an idea (albeit a rough one) about the client's overall cognitive functioning. The MMSE assesses several basic cognitive functions, including orientation, attention, recall, and receptive and expressive language. Moreover, the MMSE is easy to administer and score, and recommendations have been established for cutoff scores regarding levels of impairment. It's also not a bad idea to know something about this instrument because specialists may refer clients to you for whom MMSE scores are known.

Generally, anyone scoring over 24 on the maximum of 35 is considered to have little or no cognitive impairment, whereas scores from 17 to 23 represent some impairment. Scores below 17 are suggestive of significant impairment except where literacy or lack of formal education is a factor. Another advantage of the MMSE is that it doesn't require elaborate equipment and can be administered minutes after you've decided an assessment is worthwhile. Finally, there have been many studies done on the MMSE, which lends it a legacy of psychometric support.

If you believe that cognitive screening is appropriate, I suggest using the MMSE. If your client scores in the mid-twenties or higher, the chances are you are dealing with age-consistent memory changes. If scores are in the upper teens to mid-twenties, you should strongly consider more thorough evaluation by a clinical neuro-psychologist, geropsychologist, or neurologist. Clients in this range of functioning may also have difficulties engaging in psychotherapy. This can only be established empirically and pragmatically, that is, case by case.

Evaluating Daily Activities

A useful complement to cognitive screening is brief evaluation of daily living activities. Questions about performing such activities as managing money, using transportation, and preparing meals provide information on impairment that may be a consequence of cognitive limitations. A brief assessment of activities of daily living can follow almost seamlessly from (or precede) assessment of cognitive functioning.

Gerontologists usually demarcate basic activities of daily living (bathing, feeding, and toileting) from instrumental and advanced activities of daily living (using the telephone and cooking meals). Seniors in initial consultation for psychotherapy are much more likely to experience problems in these complex activities of daily living. I have found that asking an open-ended question ("Do you have any trouble doing things around the house?") provides me with all the information I need. I follow up on specific activities if I get an affirmative response to the open-ended query.

Here's an example. A sixty-nine-year-old married female and her husband made an appointment at the geropsychology clinic. She had been a lifelong homemaker and he was a retired insurance agent. Her husband had learned of our clinic through his bridge club. My initial telephone contact was with the husband, who indicated he was worried about his wife's increasing forgetfulness and her "clingy" behavior. His wife was unwilling to talk to our intake worker on the telephone despite encouragement and cajoling from her husband. A date was set, though there was concern that this appointment wouldn't be kept because of the wife's reluctance.

Regardless, both husband and wife showed up at the appointed time. She seemed frail; that is, she had an unsteady gait and spoke in a weak voice. She answered questions when they were posed but it was clear that she preferred to defer to her husband. In response to my opening question, "What are your reasons for coming to see me today?" even though I addressed my question directly to her, she turned her gaze to her husband in a somewhat pitiful, scared fashion. When her husband said, "You go ahead," she replied, "My memory problems." As I gathered more information on the types of problems she was experiencing, I noticed the difficulties she had with recalling recent events. For example, when I asked her if she had filled out a particular form while in the waiting room, she could not remember. Recall of remote events, such as biographical information, was no real problem for her. Because they were seeking services for memory problems, coupled with the phenomena that I observed in my interview with her, I decided to ask her if I could do a brief evaluation. "It seems like you are having some problems with your memory," I said. "I'd like to do a brief assessment that will give me a better idea about the kinds of problems you are having. Would that be OK?"

It was, and she scored 22 on the MMSE, a sort of twilight zone between clear impairment and nonimpairment. As expected, she had particular difficulty with recent-recall tasks. After giving her three words to remember, she could recall only one after a few minutes' delay and had difficulty in spelling a common word backwards. Based on my finding that there was some cognitive impairment, I requested permission to ask her about daily activities. She agreed.

I have used the Instrumental Activities of Daily Living Scale[4] as an initial session assessment tool. The IADL asks questions such as "During the past week, have you needed any help using the telephone?" and "During the past week, have you needed any help with food preparation?" Collateral sources often provide useful information when establishing daily-activity impairment levels. When you ask others who know your client well, it's important to remember the tendency of significant others to overendorse problems. In this case, however, the husband was a useful source of corroboration. I learned that my client had some difficulties with the cognitively complex activities of daily living, such as managing money and using transportation. More basic activities such as feeding and toileting were no problem for her.

My recommendation for this couple was that they get a comprehensive evaluation of the wife's neuropsychological functioning. I told them what they already knew: "You're having some troubles with your memory that are interfering with your well-being. I'd like to have someone do a complete evaluation of your memory. I'll set up the referral. In the meantime, I'd like to begin working with you on ways to get around your memory problems." They said this was exactly what they wanted to do.

It is important to remember that the MMSE or similar instruments provide only crude information and are not to be used alone for dementia diagnoses. They are screeners only. The same point is made in a recently published article, "Guidelines for the Evaluation of Dementia and Age-Related Cognitive Decline."[5] This set of guidelines provides general information on this topic, and I recommend it for the interested reader.

What to Do with the Results?

You're in your first session with an older adult, during which any number of potential factors prompt you to do a brief screening for cognitive function. You conduct it. Now, what do you do with the information you have?

If the score is in the nonimpaired range, proceed with developing a treatment plan. Specific memory complaints are probably present and worthy of attention in your treatment plan. In addition, cognitively mediated events within the session (such as loquaciousness or difficulty in understanding rapidly presented information) may occur even though cognitive screening suggests little impairment. (We talk about these issues in some depth in the chapter on interviewing strategies.) Scores suggestive of nonimpairment or minor impairment can also be used to reassure clients that "you haven't lost your mind."

What about those who score in a range suggestive of cognitive impairment? They are the bulk of those you screen, simply because you wouldn't screen them without some suspicion that something is wrong. The basic question is, Are the impairments so severe that discursive, verbal psychotherapy is likely to be too great a challenge?

If so, I would obtain consent to speak with the client's physician and concurrently attempt to schedule a thorough dementia screening. I have found most older adults to be receptive to such an arrangement, but a few are vigilant or defensive and require case-specific strategies.

For example, an African American senior was concerned this was a strategy to wrest control of his money. In essence, he felt his children were trying to get him declared incompetent so they could assume control of his estate. Because I had been in contact with one of his children in arranging the evaluation, he was wary of my intentions.

I told him, "I can see how you'd be concerned about meeting with me, but I can assure you I have no stake in the outcome of this evaluation other than to do what seems in your best interest." Further assurance and information were sufficient to assuage his concerns, but only under the condition that the evaluation be done by a different clinician! Obviously, I hadn't eliminated all of his suspicions.

We revisit the theme of cognitive status in the chapters to follow, particularly to discuss interviewing strategies. Now we turn to evaluation of medical status.

MEDICAL STATUS

Evaluating medical status during a first session with an older adult is a process of collecting information and determining the relevance of health status to diagnosis and treatment.

It is unusual for an older adult client to have no chronic medical conditions. Frequently occurring disorders are Parkinson's disease, cardiovascular disease, arthritis, respiratory disorders, stroke, pain, incontinence, digestive disorders, and just about anything else you can think of.

For example, I worked with a European American senior who had severe cardiac arrhythmia that was controlled by an implanted defibrillator. He suffered significant sleep difficulties and major depression, but because of his fragile medical conditions he could receive almost no psychotropic medication. Even in psychotherapy, it was very difficult to move beyond supportive work because of his chronic near-exhaustion and inability to devote concerted mental attention. I worked hard with him on arranging pleasurable activities (he enjoyed a glass of wine) and simple distraction techniques when negative thoughts pestered him (picturing the front entrance to every house he'd lived in, or thinking about the two funniest things that had ever happened to him). He later told me that these two techniques helped him through some of his darkest moments.

In other cases, arthritic conditions make access to our clinic difficult. Poststroke clients may have difficulties with speech that makes psychotherapy difficult. There are many age-related medical complications; our task is to make necessary modifications to facilitate engagement in a therapeutic alliance.

Gathering Medical Information

So, what does this have to do with a first session? Gathering medical information from your client is essential for planning treatment and building an alliance. Awareness of typical medical problems experienced by elders, or showing an interest in learning more about their problems, indicates to your clients a degree of competence and caring. Likewise, demonstrating sensitivity by shortening sessions with a tired client, arranging for a first-floor meeting with an arthritic client, and offering a wheelchair to the client who is out of breath because of congestive heart failure all solidify or enhance rapport.

I go about gathering information on medical status in a straightforward way; I ask the client "Are you experiencing any medical problems?" and "What medications are you taking now?" (or turn the questions to family members). I have often been dazzled by the complexity of response to these inquiries.

Asking about medications is also a good time to determine patterns of substance use. I might say, "What kind of alcoholic beverages do you enjoy?" and "When you drink, how much do you drink?" Remember that use of alcohol can interact with prescription and OTC medications. Access to a reference book on prescription medications or a pharmacist is recommended for understanding the effects of polypharmacy and substance-use interactions.

On most occasions, a consultation with the patient's physician or physicians is appropriate. I have also found physician consultation a good opportunity to bring myself up to date as to how a medical disorder or its treatment is relevant to the client's presenting problems. Most clients and physicians welcome such collaborative work. Here are some examples of the sort of questions and follow-up I might ask during a first session:

- "How much does your Parkinson's affect your day-to-day activities? Do you experience any side effects to the medication you take for it?"

- "Have you been told the size and location of the stroke you had? Did you get depressed after your stroke? What medications are you now taking as a result of your stroke?"

- "How long have you experienced arthritis? How does it affect you? Is it a source of constant pain? Does it interfere with your sleep? Do you take anti-inflammatory or pain or sleep medications?"

Specific information about medical conditions often experienced by older adults is beyond the scope of this chapter. Nonetheless, being an optimally effective psychotherapist to an older adult clientele requires one to be knowledgeable of medical conditions and their treatment.

NEED FOR SOCIAL SUPPORT

Over the years, I have become increasingly aware of the importance of social support. For older clients, a social support system is a buffer to ill effects and a facilitator of recovery.[6] As you know, social support is supplied not only by family but also by religious institutions, clubs, neighbors, friends, and professionals among others. Research on this topic[7] has also identified types of social support:

- Affective support (providing understanding and empathy)

- Instrumental support (helping out with things)

- Informational support (providing information and advice)

Here is a question I might pose to explore each respective area:

- "When you get lonely, do you have people you can talk to?"

- "If you were unable to do something, are there people you could call on to help you?"

- "Is there someone you can rely on for good advice?"

Social support is not always positive, as when people are intrusive, controlling, or pursuing their own interests. This phenomenon has been termed, oxymoronically, "negative social support." When interviewing an older client, get a sense of the types of social support they receive, if it is enough support for them, and the balance of positive and negative social support.

DIAGNOSIS

At the conclusion of a first session, most clinicians are ready to make at least a provisional diagnosis. I use the singular term *diagnosis* when in fact the plural term *diagnoses* is apt, given the high co-occurrence of mental disorders. Like many clinicians, I am ambivalent about diagnosis.

Nonetheless, my workday seems to swirl about my ambivalence. Until recently, I taught our graduate level course on psychopathology, which included the DSM-IV[8] as a textbook. My research program includes painstaking attempts to derive reliable depressive syndrome diagnoses, in which are included incidence of lifetime depression based on sketchy, retrospective reports covering sixty-plus years. Finally, I provide insurers and clients with diagnoses as part of the outpatient treatment I conduct. The point is, ambivalent though I may be, professional activities propel me to the practice of diagnostic categorization. Therefore I'll first point out what I see as the good and finish with the problems of diagnosing older clients.

Advantages

One of the primary functions of diagnosis is to promote communication. If I tell you a client evidences a delusional disorder, you immediately know something about the client. Diagnoses are useful in professional communication, both among mental health specialists and across health care disciplines. For example, some primary care physicians, with whom I have worked in providing services to older clients, seem especially comfortable with medical model nosology.

For example, written or oral communication of "recurrent major depressive episode in partial remission" is sure to impress the most die-hard of diagnostic fans (even more so if it is accurate). My opinion is that the DSM series has done very useful service in terms of facilitating research and professional communication.

If professional communication were the only function served by diagnosis, my ambivalence would run even deeper. However, I have also seen diagnosis, or more aptly a diagnostic label, provide tremendous relief for some older clients. I recently worked with a sixty-seven-year-old European American man who had suffered from "nerves" all his adult life. He described his problem this way: "I get shaky and my blood pressure goes up when someone is watching me do something, like signing the form when I use my credit card." His anxiety was particularly acute when he was asked to speak before an audience. Worse, he would worry and fret for days when he knew he was going to have his blood pressure taken or be asked to speak during church services. "If I knew I had to say something in church, I probably wouldn't go that day," he said.

Then I informed him: "I'm pretty sure you're experiencing what we call an anxiety disorder. In fact, I think the diagnosis is probably social phobia. Here are the symptoms that describe this problem." I recited the criteria for social phobia to him, and he seemed surprised by how they matched his problems. It was as if a load had been lifted. He indicated that he had shared his problem with several health care professionals over the past fifty years but that no diagnosis—or, more importantly, treatment—had been provided. He said, "I've told people about this problem before, but they just told me not to worry."

Moreover, he felt as if his complaints were addressed dismissively. True to his history of social anxiety, he was concerned that I too would dismiss his problem as "normal" (or worse, as "crazy and idiotic"). It was as if giving a name, a professional label no less, to his suffering was a source of liberation. I could almost hear him think to himself, *Finally, someone understands it.* This client was also relieved to know that many other people have problems very similar to his, that empirically supported psychosocial treatments existed, and that yours truly knew this stuff!

I've seen similar stories unfold for older clients suffering from chronic dysthymia or even major depression. Years of discomfort could have been avoided or at least diminished if they or someone else had given their problem a name and a treatment.

Providing a tentative diagnosis at the end of the initial session has been a positive in almost all cases in which I was able to do so. When providing an early diagnosis, I find it helpful to go over the DSM criteria so that my client can share in the diagnostic process. Sometimes this is not possible in an initial session, because of time constraints given all the other events taking place or because I'm simply unable to render a diagnosis. My approach to psychotherapy includes a strong commitment to collaboration and psychoeducation; thus, involving the client in my diagnostic decision making is consistent with this stance. The typical response of clients has been "Yes, that's me."

There's a final reason I like providing a diagnosis for my clients during the first session. Increasingly, the literature on psychotherapy research is providing clinicians with empirically supported treatments for particular disorders.[9] These treatments have manuals that can guide implementation and provide structure. For example, I have often used the cognitive-behavioral therapy manual developed by Elizabeth Yost and her colleagues[10] when treating depressed older adults. As I write this book, I am using a manual for the treatment of generalized anxiety disorder among older adults.[11] My take is, Why reinvent the wheel?

Lest you think all things are rosy, I'll note that providing diagnosis is not always smooth. The cases in which diagnosis has been less positive relate to cognitive impairment. Most clients and family members are quite aware of cognitive deficits, but in a few instances I have worked with families in denial. For instance, I remember one family believing their father was "faking" cognitive impairment because he had been ornery for most of his life. My initial-session observations suggested substantial impairment—put differently, moderate dementia. My diagnostic impression and recommendation for further evaluation did not play well with the family. Despite a few less-than-positive experiences with offering diagnoses to families, I recommend that you share this information with clients. My belief is that they deserve this information.

Disadvantages

For me, diagnosis becomes dirty business when it is driven by third parties, namely insurers and managed behavioral health care. I have often found myself providing a diagnosis when it just didn't fit or I could see no benefit to so doing other than financial. Welcome to the real world, right? Well, I still don't like it.

For example, I've worked with older adults for whom a diagnosis of a "V" code would be right on the nose, but not on the money. The V codes are "other conditions that may be a focus of clinical attention" and include issues such as relational problems, bereavement, or phase-of-life problem. The trouble is that these codes are sometimes not considered "medical conditions," or some other such nonsense. In such circumstances, clinicians sometimes provide an adjustment disorder or "not otherwise specified" disorder geegaw. I've found these latter diagnoses to have practically a zero communicability quotient to both clients and colleagues. This forces many of my colleagues into the game of "Here's what I'll put on this form, but what we'll work on is. . . ."

The other bad side to diagnosis as I see it concerns confidentiality. A few—and only a few—seniors with whom I have worked had real discomfort with the idea of others knowing about their mental health diagnosis. The "others" include benefits offices, past and present employers, the government, and staff at their physician's office. Whether these concerns are grounded is not the issue, because the client's concern is real and present. When this situation arises, I try to resist blowing sunshine my client's way and instead tell them that once the information on diagnosis and treatment leaves my office I have no control. Conversely, I also let them know that heretofore I've had no clients complain about outside breaches of confidentiality. Though I have never had this happen, some colleagues tell me of circumstances in which clients prefer to pay cash rather than have their information leave the building. To date, my clients have weighed the cost-benefit ratio and have concluded they'd rather let Medicare and secondary insurers pay!

Early assessment can be very important for older clients because the degree of cognitive change or severity of medical conditions has a bearing on the type of treatment offered the client. Some know-how in administering common mental-status instruments and knowing some about common medical conditions experienced by seniors make first-session assessment and diagnosis more profitable. Accurate knowledge in these domains enables you to adopt a therapeutic stance that is most conducive to forming a productive alliance. To this topic we now turn in Chapter Four.

Notes

1. Scogin, F., Storandt, M., and Lott, C. L. "Memory Skills Training, Memory Complaints, and Depression in Older Adults." *Journal of Gerontology*, 1985, *40*, 562–568; Scogin, F., Prohaska, M., and Weeks, T. E. "The Comparative Efficacy of Self-Taught and Group Memory Training for Older Adults." *Journal of Clinical Geropsychology*, 1998, *4*, 301–314.

2. Gilewski, M. J., Zelinski, E. M., and Schaie, K. W. "The Memory Functioning Questionnaire for Assessment of Memory Complaints in Adulthood and Old Age." *Psychology and Aging*, 1990, *5*, 482–490.

3. Folstein, M. F., Folstein, S. E., and McHugh, P. R. "Mini-Mental State: A Practical Method for Grading the Cognitive State of Patients for the Clinician. *Journal of Psychiatric Research*, 1975, *12*, 189–198.

4. Lawton, M. P., and Brody, E. "Assessment of Older People: Self-Maintaining and Instrumental Activities of Daily Living." *Gerontologist*, 1969, 9, 179–185.

5. American Psychological Association. "Guidelines for the Evaluation of Dementia and Age-Related Cognitive Decline." *American Psychologist*, 1998, 53, 1298–1303.

6. Krause, N. "Life Stress, Social Support, and Self-Esteem in an Elderly Population." *Psychology and Aging*, 1987, 2, 349–356; Malone Beach, E. E., and Zarit, S. H. "Dimensions of Social Support and Social Conflict as Predictors of Caregiver Depression." *International Journal of Psychogeriatrics*, 1995, 7, 5–38.

7. Barrera, M., Sandler, I., and Ramsey, T. "Preliminary Development of a Scale of Social Support: Studies on College Students." *American Journal of Community Psychology*, 1981, 9, 435–447.

8. American Psychiatric Association. *Diagnostic and Statistical Manual of Mental Disorders*. (4th ed.). Washington, D.C.: American Psychiatric Association, 1994.

9. Chambless, D. L., and others. "An Update on Empirically Validated Therapies." *Clinical Psychologist*, 1996, 49, 5–14.

10. Yost, E. B., Beutler, L. E., Corbishley, M. A., and Allender, J. R. *Group Cognitive Therapy: A Treatment Approach for Depressed Older Adults*. New York: Pergamon, 1986.

11. Stanley, M. A., Beck, J. G., and Glassco, J. D. "Generalized Anxiety in Older Adults: Treatment with Cognitive Behavioral and Supportive Approaches." *Behavior Therapy*, 1997, 27, 565–581.

4

The Alliance

Psychotherapists from varying orientations typically agree on few things when it comes to psychotherapy. But one thing that almost everyone does agree on is that the alliance is critical to successful psychotherapy. Recent years have seen a tremendous upsurge in research on this topic, and most of it converges on the finding that an early, strong alliance is probably the best predictor of successful treatment outcomes. In this chapter, I consider some ways to build a productive alliance with older clients. The initial session is arguably the most important one as far as building an alliance, so I'll talk about some first-session strategies that work.

WHAT IS AN ALLIANCE?

When we talk about an alliance in psychotherapy, most of us have a general idea of what is meant. Nonetheless, it might be helpful to look at a general definition of alliance to better appreciate this construct. Louise Gaston[1] proposed a four-part definition:

1. The working alliance, or the client's capacity to work purposefully in therapy

2. The therapeutic alliance, or the client's affective bond to the therapist

3. The therapist's empathic understanding and involvement

4. Agreement between client and therapist on the treatment goals and tasks

Interestingly, most research indicates that the client's perspective on the alliance, rather than the therapist's, is more predictive of outcome. That is, client ratings on the dimensions indicated in the list above tend to be more predictive of improvement than the same ratings made by the therapist. I offer this bit of information as a reminder that we need to be humble in our evaluations of the therapeutic alliance, for it is the client who knows best!

So, what can we do to build a strong alliance with a senior in an initial session? In this chapter I focus on the affective aspects of alliance as well as transference and countertransference. In the next chapter, on interviewing strategies, I attend to the topics of working alliance and client-therapist agreement on goals.

AFFECTIVE ASPECTS OF THE ALLIANCE

The affective bond you develop with an older client in a first session is important not only to the eventual success of treatment but also to the satisfaction you experience as a psychotherapist. Doesn't it feel good when you come out of a first session feeling you and the client have positive feelings toward one another? Conversely, I also know the nagging uncertainty when I'm not sure my client feels too positively toward me and I'm having a hard time liking the person. Let's talk about some things that can foster this important component of the alliance.

Respect

Respect for our clients is a therapeutic axiom. This seems so much the core of human decency that it hardly bears discussion. We are taught from an early age to respect our elders—yet we are bombarded with societal messages to the contrary. As psychotherapists, we have to reconcile these messages. How does a therapist (typically younger and in a position of authority) demonstrate respect for a client (typically older and in need)?

As mentioned earlier, one concrete way we try to communicate respect at our clinic is to address clients as "Mr.," "Mrs.," "Dr.," or whatever the case may be. Most clients, at some point, ask that they be addressed less formally. However, it is their call.

Another concrete thing that we do to demonstrate respect is observe our older clients arrive at the clinic for their initial visit, and walk with them from their car. Certainly, not all clients arrive by car; in fact, you may see them in a long-term care facility or even in their home. Respect in these circumstances may be demonstrated by asking permission to enter your client's room or home. For example, I remember supervising a graduate student who was seeing an older African American man who was living in a nursing home. We were careful to call ahead before the therapist went for the meeting, because the client felt it important to put on his best clothes before his "special visitor" arrived. The therapist trainee addressed him as "Mr.," and she always knocked before entering his room. These relatively small actions meant a lot to this man, who often felt diminished by the behavior of the nursing home staff. He may have been frail, but he was proud.

Our clinic also has a stairway leading to its entrance, and we are careful to assist wobbly clients. We keep on reserve a wheelchair for those clients for whom the walks to and from the parking lot are too much. As I write this, I'm reminded of a seventy-eight-year-old retired secretary I saw a few years back, who had spent much of her life being taken care of and pampered by her husband, whom she revered. His unexpected death was devastating. I remember her deep sense of appreciation when I would escort her down the stairway and to her car, taking time to stay with her so that I could close her car door. I believe these simple acts did much to create an affective bond (the second part of Gaston's definition), that is, a sense of closeness and caring in our relationship. Her heartfelt thank-yous as I closed the door gave me a good feeling that lasted for hours.

Another rather simple way to convey respect for seniors is to be on time. I have noted that older clients tend to be extraordinarily prompt and in fact are often chagrined when they are late. This punctuality is a cohort effect, no doubt, but one that deserves reciprocity. Interestingly, I have had older clients express some pleasant disbelief that sessions do begin on time, given the interminable waits required in some physicians' offices. The same holds true for older clients at community mental health clinics, who are often of lower socioeconomic status. An older person left sitting in a waiting room not only gets tired but is also given the message, "Your time is less important than our time."

Likewise, we demonstrate respect by being prepared and organized. Let me digress for a moment. As a supervisor, I often countersign progress notes written by therapist trainees. Most trainees find the "SOAP" format a useful heuristic: subjective, objective, assessment, plans (or something like that). I usually find myself scanning the "SOA" but focusing on the "P." What will be done next time? What do you (the therapist trainee) need to do between now and then? In the case of a first session, you come prepared with ideas about what you wish to cover given what you already know about your client-to-be. For example, if I know my client has trouble with anxiety, I might take an anxiety inventory to the session to use if appropriate. If I know my client would probably benefit from relaxation training, I bring in a relaxation script or a relaxation tape for the senior to use before session number two.

A therapist who comes to a session with a plan demonstrates respect very tangibly. Seniors especially value preparedness and organization, as these characteristics tend to fit with values that predominate among this cohort. As mentioned earlier, providing a written plan helps older adult clients anticipate the flow of the session. This has the added benefit of keeping the client and therapist more on track.

Projecting Competence

A corollary to preparation is to be knowledgeable, or willing to learn, about issues of importance to older adults. Reading this book is evidence that you are respectful of the privilege of working with seniors. I know that it helps in alliance building when I can demonstrate, during an initial session, knowledge of issues of aging. For example, if I can discuss with a client who is concerned about memory the differences between age-consistent changes and dementia, I sense a rise in my client's appraisal of my competence. It is the same sense of assurance we all feel when we visit a specialist, whether it is an orthopedist specializing in the knee or a mechanic who works only on front-end suspension. Even if you are not a specialist, which most readers of this book are not, willingness to learn is also a sign of respect.

If a senior comes in for an initial session today and presents with depression symptoms secondary to pancreatic cancer, I'd first tell him I don't know much about his particular cancer but want to hear what he knows. Then, I'd get permission to talk with his oncologist or primary care doctor. Finally, I'd read up. This probably all makes good sense and is what you'd do with any client. But let's take it a little further. What do you know about the Great Depression (not to be confused with Major Depression)? What do you know about living conditions and parenting practices during the 1920s and 1930s? What were the prevailing moral and social values during the 1950s and 1960s, the years during which many of today's seniors were raising their children? Let your clients teach you; they generally love to talk about their experiences. Wonderful rapport builders are such questions as "Tell me what it was like for you during WWII" or "Tell me about how your parents raised you" or "What are some things I need to know about being a Cuban American in the 1950s?"

I've heard that a person working with seniors has to be part historian, and I think it's true. Meaningful efforts to appreciate issues unique to older adults send a strong message of respect and competence and no doubt contribute to developing a therapeutic bond.

Communicating Empathically

Listening to your client—really listening—is a fundamental process in psychotherapy. By listening we develop and share empathy, show interest, and demonstrate our appreciation for what ails our clients and how they'd like things to be better. Thus, listening is an essential process in alliance building. If we as therapists are listening, it means that someone is talking—the client!

During an initial session, much of the time is spent in the clients' telling their stories and therapists making sure they're getting it. Active listening is a fundamental building block on which empathic resonance is built. Communicating your understanding of both the content and feeling that a client is sharing with you is, in my opinion, a necessary condition for a therapeutic alliance. Empathic listening my be particularly important for older-old and oldest-old adults. These individuals may be unaccustomed to people *really* listening to them. They may have sensory impairments or cognitive impairments that make communication difficult. You, as a therapist, demonstrate tremendous respect when you work at communicating with someone, when most people don't.

For example, I remember supervising a case in which a trainee was seeing a sixty-two-year-old, second-generation, German American male client for the first time. The client was talking about his frustration in not being able to get out as he used to. This was because his wife was severely demented and he worked "a thirty-six-hour day" (an apt description of the workload of anyone caring for a demented person). The therapist said: "That sounds like hard work. You must feel lonely." The client experienced a poignant emotional catharsis at that moment. His therapist had understood him in a way others had not perceived or had been unable to share with him.

The process of communication goes smoothly for most older clients, but for some it can be derailed. You've probably experienced it: a senior begins to talk with you about something, which leads to something else, and something else, and so on. I first heard this described as the issue of loquaciousness by one of the pioneers in geropsychology, Powell Lawton.[2]

When you are chatting with an older relative or a neighbor, this process is not too big a deal, and quite frankly the stream of association often leads to the most interesting of stories. During a first session, however, this can present a problem. For example, I have found myself as a therapist listening to an older client wend through an associative node. At some point, I realize I've lost track of the topic being addressed and I'm a little flummoxed as to where we are and where we should go. Managing loquaciousness is, in my opinion, crucial to developing an alliance. We must be respectful of the client's tendency to engage in this behavior, because I believe it is primarily a result of age-related changes in cognitive functioning. Whereas younger adults have strong inhibitory controls that restrain interfering or distracting stimuli, older adults have diminished inhibitory processes that allow distracting associations to divert cognitive processes.

For example, you ask, "How have things been between you and your daughter the past week?" In response your client says, "Oh, my daughter had a wreck at an intersection near our house that we go through every day. . . ." This in turn leads to "They really need to do something about that before someone gets hurt; I've nearly had a bunch of wrecks there. . . ." This then leads to a discussion of the client's safe driving habits: "Did I tell you I've decided not to drive at night any more?" You started out curious about how things were going in a particular relationship and you end up hearing about your client's difficulty with night driving. All this is seamless, mind you. Some might interpret this as defensiveness (which it could be), or loneliness, as in older people liking to talk because they don't have visitors. This is also a plausible explanation. However, a parsimonious and fundamental explanation is the breakdown in cognitive inhibition.

My point is that loquaciousness is primarily an avolitional activity. Those clients who show this pattern probably do so rather frequently. This can be frustrating for us as therapists, but it is important that we keep in mind the etiology of the behavior. Gentle redirection with a reflective comment is a useful strategy to manage talkativeness. In the example I've just given, as the client starts to talk about the unsafe intersection it is a signal to redirect: "That's too bad about the fender bender. Sounds like something needs to be done about that intersection. Tell me about some other interactions you had with your daughter this week." I would be tempted to say, "Let's get back to talking about your daughter." However, what does this add, other than to show some frustration on my part? During an initial session, in which you do not yet have a good handle on what is driving loquacity, the default explanation should be cognitive disinhibition. Patience in managing such situations goes a long way toward building an alliance.

TRANSFERENCE AND COUNTERTRANSFERENCE

The bond between client and therapist is one of the vital dimensions of the alliance. Two processes that can help or hinder development of this bond are the automatic reactions you and your client have toward one another. I use the terms *transference* and *countertransference* in this section with some reservation, since they have specific technical meanings within the psychoanalytic literature. I use these terms to describe the conscious and unconscious reactions we have to people based on their characteristics. These reactions may have some connection to early object relations (primary relationships during early childhood) but they can also be shaped by society and adult interactions. Let's talk about some of the reactions that can occur in initial-session work with seniors, beginning with transference.

Transference: Client Reactions

The most frequently discussed transference among older adults is perceiving the therapist as their adult child. This is propelled by the modal configuration of an older client and a younger therapist; indeed, some of the therapist trainees I have supervised feel this to be more like a grandchild-grandparent transference. I would assume that as the stimulus value decreases (that is, the more your age approximates that of the client) these reactions diminish. (Come to think of it, I've been told, "None of your business, sonny boy" in response to questions about changes in libido—though this has been the case with diminishing frequency over the past twenty years. Uh . . . hmm . . . excuse me; where was I? Oh, yes: transference.)

As I mention in earlier chapters, the relationship of older client and adult child is the focal point of many issues. Thus, the ramifications of this transference reaction are varied. For instance, if a client perceives your efforts to gently redirect him back to the topic at hand as controlling, and he has a child who he feels is unduly meddling, there is the possibility of a negative transference reaction. As you know, this may be happening beneath radar detection, so that neither participant is aware of what is unfolding.

Something very similar occurred in a case I treated recently. A sixty-five-year-old depressed male client was very critical of his forty-two-year-old adult daughter, who he felt was not paying enough attention to him and his wife. This retired attorney would often say "We made a lot of sacrifices to give her a better life than we had; I get teed off that she's so busy she can't give us a hand more often." Later in the session I asked him, "What are some things you might be willing to do to improve the relationship with your daughter?" I could almost feel myself being fused with the daughter in his mind, as someone who did not give enough (not agreeing that the daughter was totally at fault) but asked for more (what can you, the client, do to change the situation?). His countenance became sterner and he was a bit short with me throughout the remainder of the session. Unfortunately, I was unable to repair this rupture, and he did not return for further sessions. In hindsight, I wish I had waited until a solid relationship had been formed before I asked him this question. At the time it seemed innocent.

Fortunately, my experiences with transference reactions have been mostly positive. I think this is particularly true for reactions during an initial session. My wife, who is also a clinical geropsychologist, has told me she "sets the alliance hook" when during the first session she senses that her client is responding to her as a daughter. The alliance hook is my way of saying that a bond has been developed that is likely to carry the therapy through the rough times. My own reactions have been similar, particularly when I'm the "good son," a role I enjoy (discussion of countertransference to come later!). The good son or daughter does the things I mentioned earlier in the chapter: he or she is respectful, punctual, prepared, and competent.

When this reaction occurs, there is often a sense that the therapist is being taken care of by the client—parenting, if you will, of the therapist. For example, I can recall mentioning to seniors that I was feeling a little ill or that one of my children was sick and then almost being brought to tears by their concern and compassion. As a therapist, I feel the relationship with an older client is imbued with the qualities of a special relationship, one that only a parent and an adult child could have.

These positive transference reactions do much to build an alliance, and I have frequently seen indicants of the reactions during an initial session:

- Asking about your family

- Being concerned about "keeping you late"

- Expressing patience when you stumble over wording or have trouble explaining something

- Agreeing on goals for treatment

- Becoming visibly relaxed

- Disclosing openly

- Thanking you for understanding the situation

- Reaching out to you in an affectionate touch

A supportive, empathic relationship can fill a void in the lives of many clients. This may be especially true for those who have lost loved ones or been relocated to structured living arrangements.

Alas, there are also dangers to these reactions. Clients may perceive their relationship with you as too much like a friendship (or kinship with son or daughter) and not enough as a professional one. For example, I have had several clients who ask me to come over and share a meal with them; one senior earnestly asked me to go on a cruise with her and her husband. I told her, "Thanks, but that's probably not a good idea because I couldn't be your therapist anymore because I'd be your friend. Therapists can be friendly but not a friend" (not to mention that the licensing board might not look favorably on this dual relationship).

Clients may also expect reciprocal self-disclosure, which is generally not a good idea. For example, I have had clients ask me about problematic situations I experience with my own older parents and sister, and then expect more specifics about the situations than I feel it is best to offer. I respond: "I don't feel comfortable going into too much detail about that because it puts too much focus on me and away from you. Let's talk about some of the ways you can make your relationship better."

Finally, clients may expect special considerations such as extra time or telephone calls. I typically experience these reactions not as manipulative but more a result of the boundary with the therapist/friend becoming a bit blurred. With that in mind, I find it comfortable to say something like, "I can talk with you if something is going wrong and you're really upset, but otherwise I'd like to keep our conversations to the times we have scheduled. I enjoy talking with you and I appreciate that you like to visit with me, but I have other appointments to keep." To adequately address these complications, we must confront our countertransference reactions to older adults (a topic to which I turn shortly).

As an aside, one phenomenon that I observe only with older clients is offering food. I remember supervising a graduate student who was doing a memory training group for elders. The group had great cohesion, and they saw their leader as the "good son." One client brought a blueberry pie to one of the sessions and absolutely refused to accept no for an answer from the graduate student. We debated about what to do with the pie, as we continued to look at it with mouths watering . . . and then we ate it! What a delicious pie that was. I encouraged my supervisee to tell her how much we enjoyed the pie but to tell her that it would probably be best not to bring food—her attendance was reward enough!

In summary, transference reactions among older adults tend to manifest themselves in a direction opposite to that which is a part of clinical lore (the client reacting to the therapist as if to a parental figure). With seniors, the manifestation is more likely to be the client reacting to the therapist as an adult child. This is usually a catalyst to alliance building, but watch out for those blueberry pies!

Countertransference: Therapist Reactions

Just as our clients have automatic reactions to us, so do we have automatic reactions to them. In classic terms, countertransference reactions tend to center on responding to clients as if they are an early object relation or parental figure. As I outlined in the introduction to transference reactions, I use a broader definition of *transference* that entails almost all the automatic reactions based on the characteristics of the client. Countertransference reactions can prove to be impediments to alliance building and thus are worthy of vigilant scrutiny.

I use the term *good son* in this chapter; I'd consider the good son (or daughter) reaction in terms of countertransference. A therapist in the role of good daughter is respectful, knowledgeable, and humble. These are good characteristics of a therapist, no doubt, but I find it more difficult to confront or advance exploration of painful topics if I am comfortable in this role. This, of course, is not unique to psychotherapy with older adults, but it might be exacerbated by the unwitting reluctance to confront anyone to whom we are a good son. The bottom line is that it feels good to be held in regard, but it's also important that we be reflective about our reactions whenever we are being a good son or daughter.

Another common reaction of therapists is anticipation that working with seniors is boring, frustrating, unsuccessful, and unrewarding. This reaction comes from perceptions that older adults are all frail, cognitively impaired, and extraordinarily hard-of-hearing. Therapists with these beliefs may never see an older client out of choice, but work circumstances may nevertheless compel them to do so. I observe that most clinicians lose these negative stereotypes with some exposure to older clients, but if the exposure never comes then ageist attitudes persist.

Here are some questions you may want to ask yourself:

- What image comes to mind when you are asked to imagine an older adult? An image of a frail, limited person, or an active, engaged person?

- How do you view your own aging? With some degree of fear and loathing, or with equanimity?

- Do a large percentage of older adults live in nursing homes?

- Are most older adults experiencing low quality of life?

Examining these underlying beliefs and images in yourself and in those you train and supervise may mitigate countertransference reactions. The negative reactions that I've just presented may also be the result of a deeper issue that we as therapists must acknowledge: when we work with older adults, we face the uncertainties of our own future.

For example, I saw an anxious and depressed fifty-nine-year-old retired truck driver who had a terrible relationship with his twenty-eight-year-old son, to the point that he was not allowed to see his grandchildren. "I love my grandchildren and I want them to know I love them," he said. "I'm not sure they know that now." He made repeated attempts to repair this relationship, but his son would have none of it. My client's pain was palpable. He knew he had few years left to live, on account of severe respiratory problems, and he felt a deep sense of loss and incompleteness.

"I know I wasn't much count as a father to my son," he went on, "but I want to do better as a granddaddy. I'd feel better about my life." In Erikson's terms, he was in despair. As I talked to this client, I often found myself wondering if my own life story might unfold in some way that would lead to this execrable predicament. I felt angry with the son, but I also noticed that I was having trouble with empathic attunement. I found myself thinking something to the effect of "a man reapeth what he sows." I reminded myself of the pain my client was experiencing, to keep focused on the here and now, and also cued myself to remain vigilant for countertransference thoughts and images. I also made the pledge to myself to do right by my children. As for my client, we worked on ways he could show his love to his grandchildren that did not require direct contact, such as writing letters and sending small gifts.

Older clients continuously present with issues about *our own* aging. The youth-oriented culture in which we live makes getting older a dreaded aspect of living. Seniors show us—if we wish to focus on it—that our skin will wrinkle, we'll move stiffly, and our friends will die. Indeed, older clients remind us that *we* will die. Coming face-to-face with these issues in the incredible intimacy of the therapeutic environment is more than some therapists care to deal with, I suspect. Even in therapy, we therapists may duck discussions of death or chronic illness because of the discomfort that follows, as we consider our own aging.

Here are a pair of questions you may want to ask yourself or your supervisees:

- Are you optimistic about your future, or pessimistic?

- Are you satisfied with your life and legacy to date?

Answers to questions such as these may give you some insight into countertransference reactions to older clients.

I believe countertransference reactions with seniors can be toward both parents and grandparents. I have heard therapist trainees say that an older client reminds them much of a grandparent, a great uncle or aunt, or some other older relative. I too notice these reactions. For example, I had an older African American female client who seemed to work overtime at taking care of people. This provoked memories of a relative I have who plays a similar role; my reaction, though, was muted in comparison to those deriving from experiences with my parents. I have also noted that most countertransference reactions rooted in relationships with older relatives tend to be positive, sometimes shading into wistful. As such, these reactions can contribute to alliance building during a first session and thereafter.

As I mentioned earlier in this chapter, however, one must be careful not to allow these positive feelings to becloud therapeutic activities. Can I set appropriate limits with someone who seems like my aunt, mother, or uncle? Will I lose the status of good son if I challenge my older client's dysfunctional behavior? Can I interrupt a stream of loquacity without feeling disrespectful? These are the circumstances in which we as therapists must walk a thin line.

The negative side of countertransference reactions arising from relationships with older relatives is that they can compromise one's ability to carry out aspects of the role a therapist must assume. For example, it can be difficult to offer constructive criticism, set limits, or provide advice on issues foreign to a younger therapist.

Imagine advising one of your older relatives about his or her sex life. I would certainly squirm at the Thanksgiving table when it comes to that one. The prospect of an older client asking me about the same probably provokes some feelings. These countertransference reactions are quite common and have the potential to undermine development of a working alliance.

A more pertinent example is loquaciousness. A therapist must be able to gently and sometimes repeatedly intervene during a session to maintain focus. Are you as comfortable doing this with an older client as with a younger one? Probably not, and that's OK, because I think the hesitance is born out of respect for elders—an inclination that is in most ways facilitative. Hesitation may dampen our push to "get to the issue" or "accomplish something," tendencies that some clients experience as therapist impatience or dissatisfaction with the client. In some cases, the hesitance may be driven by fear of rejection or criticism, but this is more likely a result of traditional countertransference reactions. When I experience such fear, I remind myself of the responsibility and privilege I have as a therapist to do what I think is best for my client, even if avoidance is a more comfortable option.

Nevertheless, respectfulness cannot overwhelm one's responsibility to be a competent therapist. The mark of a skillful therapist is to be aware of issues such as respectful hesitance and turn them into respectful action. For example, when you become aware that a senior is straying, what do you do? Do you say "Let's get back to the topic"? A little abrupt, maybe not consistent with respectful hesitance. Or do you listen for five minutes in hopes the soliloquy makes its way back to the initial question? That's probably too respectful. I tell many supervisees that their clients need help to stay on track. It's OK to say "We're drifting off the topic, I think. Let's go back to how your thinking made your sadness even worse." Allowing seniors to talk themselves in circles is no service. The ultimate sign of respect is to aid a client with difficulties, and this often requires us to do discomfiting things.

The alliance construct used in this chapter was developed by Louise Gaston and her colleagues. A concluding sentence to a study she and her colleagues conducted[3] is a good summary for this chapter: "A sense of being in an intimate collaborative relationship with another person may be particularly important for older depressed adults who have lost significant persons, capacities, or occupations." I too believe this to be true. Developing a warm, collaborative relationship with an older adult client can be deeply gratifying. However, we must be aware of countertransference reactions that can undermine our ability to do the harder tasks of interviewing. The next chapter is devoted to interviewing strategies for a first session.

Notes

1. Gaston, L. "The Concept of the Alliance and Its Role in Psychotherapy: Theoretical and Empirical Considerations." *Psychotherapy*, 1990, *27*, 143–153.

2. Lawton, M. P. "Functional Assessment." In L. Teri and P. M. Lewinsohn (eds.), *Geropsychological Assessment and Treatment*. New York: Springer, 1986.

3. Gaston, L., Marmar, C. R., Gallagher, D., and Thompson, L. W. "Alliance Prediction of Outcome Beyond In-Treatment Symptomatic Change as Psychotherapy Processes." *Psychotherapy Research*, 1991, *1*, 104–113.

5

Interviewing Strategies

Interviewing strategies are where the rubber meets the road as far as psychotherapy is concerned. The first-session interview forms the foundation upon which psychotherapy rests, and as such it is the key to successful treatment. In this chapter, I present some ideas about how to optimize the yield of the initial session. In previous chapters, I've discussed the importance of cognitive functioning in work with older adults. Now I'd like to talk about some interviewing strategies that may compensate for these age-related cognitive changes. In this chapter we also cover some ideas about preparing clients for psychotherapy, a topic particularly relevant for seniors. We conclude with some thoughts on involving family members.

MANAGING THE PROCESS

I believe it is important that therapists enter an initial session with a senior with a plan or a framework. For me, the framework includes getting a good idea about what the presenting problems are, discussing treatment options, and providing an orientation to the treatment that is likely to be implemented. Managing the pace at which these areas are explored is one of the major tasks facing the clinician working with older adults.

The Pace

A couple of years back I attended a presentation by Bob Knight, a clinical geropsychologist at the University of Southern California and an authority on the topic of psychotherapy and aging. During his talk, he used a phrase that, with his characteristic pith and cleverness, captured the spirit of this chapter: "Slow down the pace to speed up the process." Let's dilate these words of wisdom.

Most older adults with whom you work show some decline in working-memory capacity (covered in some detail in Chapter One). This means that the speed with which information is presented as well as the volume of information presented must be modified. For example, I have observed that if I talk at the same clip I use with colleagues, I find myself repeating or clarifying with some elders. If this occurs on many occasions, the overall process can be damaged. Consequently, I am mindful that I may need to speak slightly slower and use fewer complex and compound sentence structures.

It's easy to fall into this pattern of rapid, complex speech. As an example of how not to speak, consider this question: "When you think about this issue, just before you go to bed and after a get-together with your new friend, do you find that getting to sleep or staying asleep is more of a problem than before?" This is an extreme example, but I've heard words of a similar nature come from my mouth. Better would be any of these:

"Did you get together with your new friend?"

"Did you worry about it afterwards?"

"Did it affect your sleep like before?"

Rapid speech or complex syntax requires greater attentional resources and working-memory effort. By slowing the pace, you actually get more done. To slow down and simplify requires some patience and self-discipline, but the payoff is that time spent in clarification and repetition can be used productively in exploring issues of concern to your client or gathering useful information for clinical judgments.

Managing Impairments

There are other ways to optimize interviewing. For example, hearing impairments often interact with cognitive deficits to make communication with some seniors a challenge. My advice is to turn up the volume a little (but don't shout)—and turn up the bass. Slow down the pace of speech, as mentioned before, and enunciate clearly. Also, make sure the lighting is good so your client can clearly see your face, particularly your mouth. Sit close enough that you can be clearly seen, but not so close as to violate personal space. These small things help a senior with hearing impairment read as many of the motoric and nonverbal aspects of communication as possible. Also, minimize background noise such as voices from adjoining rooms or traffic noise from an open window. Older adults are less able to discriminate signal from noise, that is, less able to perceive the desired stimuli and inhibit undesired stimuli. Clients teach you the modifications necessary to reach optimal communication, but only if you are exquisitely attuned to the process.

In our clinic, we also make good use of multimedia. I mean multimedia in a low-tech sense. We often take a whiteboard into sessions with older adults to record the agenda for that meeting and to mark the main points covered. This serves as a memory cue for the client and reduces the burden on attentional resources. We also provide clients with a clipboard and outline of the session agenda for note taking, should they wish to have a take-home copy. This is probably more appropriate for later sessions in structured forms of psychotherapy such as cognitive-behavior therapy (CBT), but it is in keeping with the notion of helping clients compensate for diminished cognitive capacity. We also allow clients to audiotape sessions if they desire so they can replay them at home. Because tape recorders are gadgets, they can be frustrating for some older clients who don't see well or are not nimble. It might help to color code the play and rewind buttons and make sure the sound quality is good on the tape before you send them away. Giving a recording of a therapy session to a client may strike some as anathema to the sanctity of the consulting room; my rejoinder is it ain't much good if you can't recall it.

Another aide to memory for older clients is to use good pedagogy: preview it, discuss it, and review it. For example, if during the initial session I want to work on a treatment plan with a client, I say: "Now, let's talk some about what we can do to help you with this. After we've done so, we'll go over it again and then write it down so you can look at it when you're at home."

Another topic under the heading of pace and process has to do with fatigue. Some older clients are frail and easily fatigued. Some are even pretty worn out by the time they make it to your office. For these seniors, it may be worth considering *in-home treatment sessions*, a topic I take up later in this chapter. A shorter initial session should be an option for frail clients. Signs that fatigue is setting in are often pretty obvious, such as being told by the client that she is tired or seeing that she occasionally drifts off to sleep. Less obvious signs that fatigue may necessitate a shorter session are irritability or increasingly brief responses from the client. I handle circumstances like this by sharing my hypothesis about what is going on: "It seems like you might be getting a little tired." If they say yes, I say something like, "Since you're getting tired, let's stop for today and pick up where we left off next time."

I remember seeing a rural home health care recipient, an eighty-eight-year-old Hispanic, who was quite physically weak. Our treatment team (a social worker and I) had been with her for only about fifteen minutes, in her home, before she told us she was too tired to continue. This woman was very sick and clearly could not tolerate the stress of what was to her a long interview. Nonetheless, our contact was meaningful for her since she received few visitors. We said: "We're going to go now so you can get some rest. But we'll be back in two days." Her faint smile remains a vivid memory.

Often family members are active participants in treating easily fatigued clients and can advise you as to the stamina of the older adult before you begin the session. A half-hour initial session may be optimal for some clients, as opposed to the ninety-minute sessions that are used in many initial interviews. Rather than trying to pack a lot into the half-hour (or longer), I try deliberately to go slow and respect my client's limitations. Remember, slow down the pace to speed up the process.

Directive Versus Nondirective Interviewing Strategies

The initial session serves as a template for future sessions of psychotherapy. From the client's perspective, questions such as "Will my therapist be easy to talk to?" and "What will psychotherapy be like?" are in large part answered during the first session. One dimension on which such evaluations are made is the interviewing strategy adopted by the psychotherapist. A major consideration is directiveness. At one end of the directiveness continuum are structured diagnostic interviews, in which each question is scripted and the facts, nothing but the facts, are desired. At the other end are interviews that begin with the therapist silently awaiting the client's setting of the direction of the session. Neither of these would actually occur (I hope), but decisions do need to be made as to the degree of directiveness used in an initial session.

I advocate a directive first interview for seniors. I reason as I have discussed earlier: open-ended, abstract queries such as "What would you like to work on?" can lead to stream-of-consciousness unveiling among even the most cognitively intact, linear thinkers. For older clients, a directive interviewing style is usually indicated, especially in the first session. This is in keeping with the tips I offered earlier, such as having an agenda and using less complex questions. Present-day seniors may also appreciate a directive style, because this is more consistent with their expectations about what a doctor-patient interaction may be. This is not to imply that psychotherapy with older adults should generally be directive; rather, a first session that is largely guided by the therapist is usually more comfortable for seniors.

AGENDA FOR A FIRST SESSION

When I begin the first session with an older client, I verbally (and sometimes on the whiteboard as well) lay out an agenda for the first meeting.

A typical one is something like this:

1. Limits of confidentiality
2. Reasons for seeking services
3. Potential treatments
4. Therapy orientation
5. Plans

I let my client know that we'll skip around if need be, and we can talk about things that aren't on the list. I also let them know that we might not cover all these topics today because we don't want to rush. I think most older clients appreciate this degree of structure and experience it as a sign that they are being taken care of. Let me go over each of these areas in more detail.

Limits of Confidentiality

This necessary but mildly uncomfortable topic is often included in client agreement forms, but I like to briefly and matter-of-factly present it at the beginning of a first session. What I say to an older client is no different from what I say to a younger one (though maybe a little slower and lower):

> Before we start, I'd like to share some information with you. What we talk about here will stay between us. I don't talk to other people about our conversations. This is

called confidentiality. There are limits, however, to confidentiality. If I believe you are a danger to yourself or someone else, I must break our confidence and act to protect whoever's in danger. Do you have questions about that? Also, because you will be using insurance to cover your bill, I'll need to provide your diagnosis and the times we meet to Medicare and your insurance company. OK?

I cannot recall a time when a client has had a problem with this brief message. Nonetheless, it continues to feel to me like a small double bind, that is, "Talk freely with me, but watch what you say."

Interesting variants on the limits of confidentiality are the elder abuse reporting laws. Similar to child abuse laws in most states, certain professionals (including therapists) are required to report suspected cases of neglect or abuse of an older person to proper authorities. Elder abuse is most frequently committed by family members. This means that the person who might be abusing could be with the older person during the initial session. If sessions are to be conducted with persons other than your client in attendance (spouse, adult child, in-law), it is important that your legal obligations be made clear to all parties. For example, when family members or others are present for the first session, I say: "If I have reason to believe that any harm or neglect is occurring to anyone here, or to others not in this room, then I am required to take actions to protect whoever is at risk. Do you have any questions about that?"

I talk about dealing with elder abuse and neglect situations in the next chapter, on handling crises.

Reasons for Seeking Services

Next, I ask the client, "What brings you to the clinic today?" Actually, I say something more along the lines of: "I'd like to spend the bulk of our time today talking about your reasons for seeking treatment. I've talked briefly with your physician, but I'd like to hear in your words what's going on."

Most clients have rehearsed their response to this question because it is so obvious a starting place. Some older adults may not know where to start, at which point I might say: "OK, no problem, maybe I can help get us going. Your doctor said he felt as though you were nervous and tense. Can you tell me about that?"

Clients may also have difficulty defining problems. They may know that they don't feel happy or are anxious, but they have trouble being much more specific. This is particularly true for seniors with cognitive impairment. For example, it is true that we cannot eliminate an arthritic condition, but we can help an older adult cope more effectively with the pain and depression that can accompany this condition. In helping the older client define the problem, we can then talk about ways we might be able to offer assistance.

Potential Treatments

If I come up with a firm idea as to presenting problem and diagnosis, I reserve about five minutes toward the end of the session to talk about some potential treatment approaches. I am a thoroughly eclectic psychotherapist, so I feel free to mix and match. For the sake of simplicity, let me work through an example of someone who is experiencing mixed anxiety-depression disorder:

> It seems to me that you're having problems with nervousness and worry, as well as some depression symptoms. It also seems that these feelings are related to a lot of things, but much of it has to do with the financial burdens you told me about. There are a couple of treatment options, as I see it. One is to do a type of psychotherapy known as cognitive-behavioral therapy. This type of treatment has worked very well with older adults who have problems like those that you've talked about. I'll explain it more thoroughly in a minute. Another potential treatment is medication. Drugs work well in reduc-

ing the symptoms of anxiety and depression. Most doctors recommend that a combination of medication and psychotherapy is best. I could discuss this with your physician if you are interested.

Most clients have some questions or comments about the treatments: "I don't want to get addicted to drugs" or "How long will this last?" After fielding these questions ("These drugs are not addictive" and "Typically, three or four months for the psychotherapy, probably longer for the medication"), I begin an orientation to treatment.

Therapy Orientation

Number four on the agenda proposed earlier is less familiar to some readers. What I mean by therapy orientation is providing clients with general information about the process of psychotherapy—for example, the roles the therapist and client are likely to play, how long it might last, and information on the effectiveness of the treatment. Research on "role preparation" consistently shows that clients who receive this orientation tend less to drop out of treatment and are likely to achieve better outcomes.[1] In most research studies, the orientation takes place just prior to the first session and is delivered through written material or video.

I prefer to do my orientation during the first session, after I have learned something about my client and the presenting problem. I think this sort of orientation is particularly good for seniors. As a group, they usually have less contact with mental health professionals and thus less information about psychotherapy. It is also possible that they have misconceptions about psychotherapy (perhaps that it involves heavy emphasis on exploring their sexuality, or that it is incompatible with religious beliefs). For these reasons, spending about ten minutes in the first session talking about, for example, the idea that they are expected to do some talking and the therapist will do some listening should be strongly considered.

Here are some words I use in a generic orientation:

> I want to spend just a couple of minutes talking about what therapy will be like. We'll meet on a regular schedule, probably weekly, for about an hour a session. During these sessions, you and I will talk about the things you've identified as problems. For example, we might talk about ways you've put into practice what we've discussed in earlier sessions. You'll be doing a lot of the talking and I'll do a lot of listening. Together we'll come up with ideas about how to make things better. All of this will take some work on your part. Do you have questions about what therapy will be like?

Choosing to conduct the orientation toward the end of the session also allows the presentation to be tailored to fit the treatment that is likely to be offered. For example, if I believe a cognitive-behavioral treatment is indicated, I can present information on the notions of collaborative empiricism (working together to obtain information on the validity of thinking patterns), homework assignments, and psychoeducation as part of the orientation. If interpersonal therapy seems indicated, I could inform the client that we will focus on current relationship difficulties and attempt to do some problem solving. Most psychotherapy manuals have a section on how to conduct an orientation to that particular brand of therapy. One of the best I've seen is an orientation to CBT for geriatric depression.[2] My orientation for the hypothetical senior with mixed anxiety-depression is based on this model:

> OK, let's talk some about the therapy I recommend. It's called CBT and I'll show you why. [Go to whiteboard, chalkboard, or notepad and draw Figure 5.1.]
>
> CBT is based on the notion that how we think influences how we feel and react to things. These four areas are related. For example, the health side has a big influence on how we feel. Think about the last time that you

Figure 5.1. Cognitive-Behavior Therapy Orientation

Thoughts

Behaviors   Emotions

Health

had a cold or the flu. What was your mood like? Right, pretty crummy. [Draw link between health and emotions.] Now, what kind of thoughts did you have when you were sick? For example, some people might think they were never going to get better or even die. How do you think these thoughts might affect how you act? And how you feel? [Continue this activity until all four domains are connected.] So, you can see that how we act, think, feel, and react physically are connected.

Most people come to therapy because they don't feel good emotionally. [Indicate this on figure.] You came here mostly because you were feeling worried and depressed. Unfortunately, it is hard for me to directly change how you feel. You've tried that yourself, I bet. Similarly, I can't change your physiology directly, though if you decide to talk to your doctor about this we may be able to use medications to help your body recover. That leaves us two factors to work on in therapy: behavior and thoughts. This is how CBT got its name. We can work on changing your behaviors and thoughts, and what follows, we hope, is less worry and depression.

Here's an example. Suppose you were at home one night and you heard something crash in another room. If you thought, "There's a burglar in the house," how do you think you'd feel? Right, scared half to death. But what if you thought, "Oh, I left the window open and the wind blew something over." How would you feel?

Yeah, a bit frustrated and mad probably, but nowhere near as scared. What this example shows is that there are different ways to think about things, and how you think affects how you feel and behave.

(The example in the last paragraph is adapted from Beck and colleagues.[3])

I find that this process takes about ten minutes and most folks get it. As you might expect, cognitive impairment affects the pace and volume of material to be presented. Asking the client to give an example that demonstrates understanding is a good way to check on the effectiveness of your teaching.

In the final portion of my orientation, I bring home forcefully the evidence on the effectiveness of psychotherapy, being as specific as possible about the therapy I think might be implemented. For instance, in orienting a senior with generalized anxiety disorder, I would share the conclusion of a task force on empirically supported treatments[4] convened by the American Psychological Association: that CBT is a well-established treatment for this disorder. I would also present information on the percentage of people who achieve clinically significant change. Older adults may have the idea that psychotherapy might help a little but that its overall impact is rather anemic. My goal is to get the word out, to my client and to anyone else who will listen: psychotherapy is strong medicine.

Plans

The end of the first session is the time to make plans for upcoming sessions. Some of this is pedestrian—for example, when you will meet, how often, how long, payment, etc. A more substantive planning issue is to get commitment from the client to try the therapy for a set number of sessions. For the hypothetical case of mixed-anxiety, I would tell the senior that the treatment protocol is ordinarily fifteen to twenty sessions, but that we can meet for five sessions and then take stock of where we are. For other clients, much shorter treatment length is the norm and goals must be ratcheted down accordingly. If I have only three or four sessions in which to work, I would inform my client that I hope we can plant some seeds (metaphorically speaking) that the client will need to continue watering and nurturing once our brief contact is finished. I place much more value on introducing coping skills, such as relaxation, bibliotherapy, and sleep hygiene, and much less on actually developing skills in these areas. I also try to surmount whatever barriers might exist to having a reasonable number of sessions with which to conduct psychotherapy.

INVOLVING THE FAMILY

As I have mentioned in earlier chapters, involving family members is an interesting twist in working with older clients. As the degree of caregiving increases, so does the likelihood that a family member will participate in treatment. Decision making by the therapist on the structure of this involvement is most frequent during the initial session. Consider this scenario. A frail, eighty-two-year-old client is brought to an initial session by her fifty-three-year-old daughter. The mother lives with the daughter and her family, has been complaining about sadness, and seems increasingly irritable. Contacts with the client and daughter have heretofore been through clinic staff. You greet them in the waiting room and the daughter asks, "Would you like me to come with Mom?" *Hmmm, interesting question*, I say to myself. I look at Mom; she seems alert and oriented but somewhat apprehensive. Not really sure of what's up, I go with the flow and say, "OK, let's meet together."

As I lay out the agenda for the session, I tell them I would also like to spend some time with Mom alone. Thereafter, I remain attuned to factors such as the cognitive functioning of my client and the pattern of interaction between mother and daughter.

In most cases of this sort, the family member is an ally in the treatment, in terms of information and support. My inclination in

subsequent sessions is to work primarily with the older adult, but
I continue to involve the family by conferring periodically with
the family member(s) during the sessions. I try to have the senior
present during these conferences so that the client knows what is
being said.

———————

Initial-session interviewing strategies for seniors must take into
account the cognitive and physical status of the client. Efforts to
minimize the memory and attentional demands placed upon your
client are important for an optimal process. Potential compensatory
techniques include using multiple routes for presenting information,
slowing the pace and complexity of dialogue, providing a greater
degree of structure, and erring on the side of a directive initial-
session format. Involving family members in the initial session is
also a question of interviewing strategy that has no easy answer. At
the risk of oversimplifying a complex situation, I recommend
involving the family in the initial session unless you have strong
reasons not to. In the next chapter, I present ideas about how to
handle emergencies that may occur in a first session with a senior.

Notes

1. Garfield, S. L. "Research on Client Variables in Psychotherapy." In
A. E. Bergin and S. L. Garfield (eds.), *Handbook of Psychotherapy
and Behavior Change*. (4th ed.). New York: Wiley, 1994.

2. Thompson, L. W., Gallagher-Thompson, D., and Dick, L. P. *Cogni-
tive-Behavioral Therapy for Late Life Depression: A Therapist Manual*.
Palo Alto, Calif.: Older Adult and Family Center, Veterans
Affairs, Palo Alto Health Care System, 1995.

3. Beck, A. T., Rush, A. J., Shaw, B. F., and Emery, G. *Cognitive
Therapy of Depression*. New York: Guilford Press, 1979.

4. Chambless, D. L., and others. "An Update on Empirically Validated
Therapies." *Clinical Psychologist*, 1996, 49, 5–14.

6

Crisis Intervention

Older adults sometimes present problems during initial sessions that require crisis intervention. In this chapter, I talk about three specific situations that occur with seniors. The first occurs when you judge your client's cognitive impairment to be so severe as to make independent living (or perhaps, more immediately, even driving) a critical risk. This crisis can be categorized under the broad heading of competence. The second issue has to do with older clients who are depressed or hopeless. As you probably know, based on demographic status alone you have a person at-risk for suicide. We also discuss elder abuse. I close this chapter with some thoughts about helping older adults handle emergencies on their own, such as intense grieving, loneliness, and fear.

THE ISSUE OF COMPETENCE

Competence is a construct used in legal proceedings. There are criminal competencies such as whether a defendant is able to stand trial, or be executed, or waive Miranda rights. Civil competencies are of more relevance to work with older adults: ability to handle financial matters and make medical decisions, and testamentary competence (creating or changing a will). Cognitive abilities are a strong determinant of these civil competencies. We know that cognitive abilities change in late adulthood, and we also know that the dementias such as Alzheimer's are age-related. During an initial session with a senior, it may become apparent that the degree of cognitive impairment evinced by your client may compromise his ability to function competently. Ordinarily, this is not an emergency, but in at least a couple of instances it can rise to that level (say, driving an automobile or living without sufficient supervision).

Consider two responsibilities that we assume as psychotherapists. First, we have an obligation to do something if we believe a client poses a danger to self or others. Relatedly, we have a duty to protect others in cases where there is a clear threat to well-being. I should note that the legal obligations to report and act vary according to jurisdiction. You should be familiar with statutes in force where you work. For the purpose of this chapter, let's talk generally about what I consider our professional obligations.

Driving

Older adults with moderate to severe cognitive impairment may be a danger to self or others when operating a motor vehicle or living independently. This situation once arose for me. An eighty-four-year-old widowed female was referred to me. Her son was concerned about her increasing forgetfulness and personality changes. My initial session was with her alone. This rather proper and somewhat stern woman, a retired college professor, immediately presented behavior demonstrating significant cognitive impairment. She was two hours early for the appointment and parked in a no-parking zone. She was quite convinced that she had the appointment time right and that we must have gotten confused. She couldn't remember whom her appointment was with because she couldn't find the piece of paper in her purse. As I talked with her during our session, it was clear she did not fully understand why she was meeting with me. I said, "Your son wanted us to meet so I could give him and you some ideas about how to help you with your memory changes."

She said, "Why do I have to come to a shrink for that?" When I asked her if I might do a brief assessment of her memory (MMSE), she was reluctant: "I don't really want to do that . . . let's talk about something else."

So, I informally assessed her orientation and short-term memory by asking such questions as "What's your grandson's name?" and "What's today's date?" She couldn't answer these questions, though to the casual observer she might have been able to mask her impairment by virtue of her social graces. By that, I mean she responded to questions such as today's date with "Well now, *you'd* know that answer, it's more important for someone in your job to keep up with things like that."

By the end of the session, I was convinced that this client was experiencing significant cognitive impairment. My immediate concern was that she was still driving her car. I might add that this client was living in a trailer and had few financial resources. Not surprisingly, her car was in very poor condition. Because she had driven to the appointment I did not feel right in snatching her keys from her hand, but I did feel uncomfortable as she drove away. Before the end of the session, she gave me written permission to speak to her son, of whom she said, "He takes care of all my matters." Had I not gotten this permission, I would have been on the horns of a dilemma. If this had been the case, I would have phoned her to get assent to talk with her son. If she had refused, I would have had to consider if bad driving was a serious enough threat to safety to break confidentiality. To aid in this decision making, I would have consulted a trusted colleague to discuss the situation. My guess is that I would not have overridden confidentiality and would have talked to my client about my concerns at our next session.

Back to the story. I called her son right away to share my concerns about her ability to make the quick decisions and proper judgments required in safe driving. I recommended that we have a family meeting as soon as possible to discuss the driving issue.

I was less concerned about his mother's ability to take care of herself in daily matters because her son kept close tabs on her. He called or visited her almost every day. I also had the unpleasant task of informing the family that dementia of the Alzheimer's type was probably the reason for the changes in her behavior.

Managing Self-Care

A fundamental concern arises when you begin to question a client's ability to take care of herself. The case just described could have presented another first-session emergency had there been no caregiver, the role played by the son. I would have had significant concerns about the client's ability to handle the complex activities of daily living such as managing finances, preparing meals, responding to emergencies, and using the telephone. If she had not had a family caregiver (as was true with another case I supervised a few years ago), I would have requested permission to contact a family member.

In this other case, a student trainee contacted a son who was living in town but we quickly surmised he was a ne'er-do-well. We knew the client had a brother who lived in another state, so we contacted him. He somewhat reluctantly agreed to look into the situation and in fact did eventually have his sister placed in an assisted-living setting.

If there is no family to contact or my client refuses to grant permission to speak to a family member, I would strongly consider contacting a governmental agency charged with protection of adults. I would need to consider the person at risk for harm. A person with moderate to severe dementia can be a risk for self-neglect, such as improper nutrition or poor hygiene. Such people also present risk in using household appliances or operating a motor vehicle. Calls to adult protective services should result in an investigation into the situation.

Interestingly, I remember a situation of this sort arising not in my clinical work but in my neighborhood. A widow in her nineties lived a short distance from us. A retired schoolteacher, she lived in an enormous, unkempt Victorian house. Over the years, we observed her ability to take care of herself diminish as she became demented. She had a daughter who lived out of town but was not responsive to our telephone calls warning her of her mother's declining ability. The situation reached a critical juncture when we repeatedly observed our neighbor walking down the middle of our somewhat busy street on the way to visit us. It was just a matter of time until she was struck by a speeding vehicle. We finally called Adult Protective Services and reported our concerns. They were able to arrange a sitter for her and got the daughter involved in caring for her mother. We have not been favorites of the daughter, as you might expect.

MANAGING SUICIDAL ELDERS

Work with depressed seniors involves response to suicide-related crises. One way to put this in perspective is to look at Figure 6.1, which depicts suicide rates by age, race, and sex. The figure is clear: rates for older adults are relatively high, particularly for older men, and dramatically so for older white men. Though I try to be vigilant about assessing suicidal risk in all clients, these epidemiological data prompt me to be especially alert with depressed older white men. Suicidal assessment should be considered a necessary part of an initial session with all clients, and we should be prepared to act based on what we find. As therapists, we assume an obligation to protect our clients; in the case of suicidal clients, we must protect our clients from themselves.

An interesting yet disturbing research finding is that a rather high percentage of people who committed suicide had recently visited their medical provider. Around 75 percent of those committing suicide had conferred with a doctor within the month; 20 percent had visited within the past twenty-four hours.[1] These data remind us to be vigilant to the potential for suicide in our clients. Additionally, several of my colleagues and I have advocated routine use of geriatric depression screening in primary care settings.[2] Perhaps such activity would help prevent some of the unneeded suicides among older adults.

Figure 6.1. Suicide Rates by Five-Year Age Groups, Race, and Sex: United States, 1989.

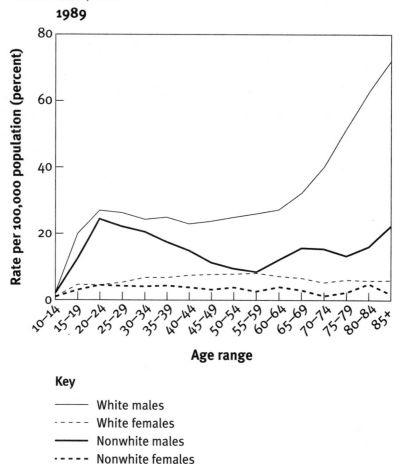

Source: J. L. McIntosh, J. F. Santos, R. W. Hubbard, and J. C. Overhelser, *Elder Suicide: Research, Theory, and Treatment.* Copyright © 1994 by the American Psychological Association. Reprinted with permission.

Assessment

I want next to discuss the situation that arises when you discover during your first session that a client has suicidal thoughts or plans. I usually find it best to ask "the suicide question" in the following sequence:

1. "How would you describe your mood over the past couple of weeks?"
2. "Have you lost interest in things recently?"
3. "Have you had thoughts that life is not worth living?"

If I get nondepressive responses to these questions, I feel confident that suicide risk is low—or at least being well guarded. In my experience, the response to the suicide question is usually a clear-cut and immediate no or else something that raises my concerns. Here are some examples of the latter:

- "I think my family might be better off without me."

- "With my ailments and pain, I don't look forward to the next day."

- "It sometimes feels like my situation is hopeless."

If I get such responses, or if at any other time during the interview I sense my client is telling me that life is not worth living or that the senior is experiencing hopelessness, I ask more questions to determine the seriousness of the suicide potential.

Let's take the "My family would be better off without me" statement. Follow-up questions might be

- "How often do you find yourself thinking this?"

- "How long have you felt this way?"

- "Are there particular situations when you find yourself thinking that your family would be better off without you?"

This type of question gives me some idea about the frequency and intensity of the thinking pattern. The next—and most important—question would be, "When you find yourself thinking like this, do you ever have thoughts of hurting yourself?" Most depressed older clients with whom I have worked indicate that they do not have such thoughts, and even if they did they would not consider acting on them for religious reasons or because of the pain it would cause their family. In these cases, I make a mental note to ask them about this again before they leave the office and to make sure they know to call me or a backup person, perhaps a crisis line or a colleague on-call, if their suicidal thoughts become more active.

Some seniors indicate that they have active suicidal ideation. For example, many of us have had clients say, "Yeah, I've had thoughts of killing myself, but I don't think I'd do it right, I'd probably end up paralyzed and worse off than ever." Others say that they would not take their own life because of the harm it would do to their family or because it is against their religious values.

Imminence and lethality are the next areas of inquiry for me. I might ask

- "Have you made any plans about how you might hurt yourself?"

- "How would you try to kill yourself?"

- "Do you have firearms (. . . medications, carbon monoxide)?"

Action

If I determine that my older client has suicidal thoughts but they are not well-formulated, imminent, or lethal, I am likely to spend a great portion of the time in that session extracting a commitment from my client. It would be that the senior would not act on these thoughts without contacting me, a crisis line, a friend, or a family member. If given permission, I would also contact family members or caregivers about my concerns and try to set up a support-and-surveillance system. I would also schedule a second session with my client to follow within a few days of the first. In the meantime, I would be a bit apprehensive.

Here's a case example. A seventy-three-year-old, widowed, African American man was referred to me for treatment of depression. The referral came from a fellow churchgoer who was concerned about the client's behavior: "He's been real sad and crying a lot." My client was indeed experiencing an episode of major depression. He was also almost destitute, having no pension or savings, and living on Social Security benefits. To make matters worse, he was a lifelong smoker and had had one cancerous lung removed. His health was poor and failing. However, he showed no evidence of cognitive impairment.

As I asked him questions about depressive symptoms, I learned that he had experienced suicidal thoughts. "I think life's not worth the living every day of the week," he said. "I have to worry about having enough money to pay bills, and I can hardly take care of myself, I'm so give out. People at church try to help me but I'm just a burden to 'em."

I asked him if he had made any suicidal plans.

"Not yet, " he said.

"I'm not sure what you mean. . . ."

"Just means I don't want to do it, but if things don't get some better I'm not sure I can carry on."

My client's responses suggested that I needed to work out a crisis-management plan. My guess was that he was not going to be feeling much better over the next few days or weeks, so the potential for escalation of suicidal ideation was present.

"I'm a little concerned about your thoughts that life is not worth living," I told him. "I know that sometimes it may not seem like it, but I think you do have reasons to be alive. When you're depressed, it is hard to see the positives. I'm committed to helping you get over your depression so you can enjoy life more. So, I want to try to work out a deal with you. Between now and the next time we meet, would you be willing to call me if you start feeling worse?"

"OK, but I don't have a telephone. I use my neighbor's."

"That's all right, as long as you can be sure to get to it if you start feeling suicidal."

"I will."

I got the impression that he felt good about my crisis-management plan, as if it indicated that I really cared enough to look out for him. I think our working alliance was further enhanced when I discussed with him the possibility of starting on an antidepressant and having the public health department look into the possibility of home health care.

The final scenario is when an older client, usually depressed, has both a plan and intent. In cases of this sort that I can recall, I pursued in-patient hospitalization for my client. This is most smoothly accomplished when the client recognizes the need for such treatment and is a willing participant. More troubling are those circumstances where involuntary hospitalization is the last option. In Alabama, this is typically handled by getting a client to the emergency room. This usually means persuading the person to go to the ER voluntarily or be brought there by law enforcement. At the emergency room, the client is evaluated by a mental health professional and a determination is made as to whether a seventy-two-hour emergency commitment is warranted. A probate hearing is conducted for continued involuntary hospitalization. The nuances of this procedure vary from state to state and are a matter of civil law. It is important that you have some knowledge of these procedures, should you work with a high-risk suicidal senior.

It is important to maintain rapport and support with your client as you undertake involuntary hospitalization. You will probably continue as the person's therapist after hospitalization, and in some cases you may provide therapy to your client while he is in the hospital. Offer thorough explanation of why you are pursuing this option and what the steps are. My experience is that most people opt for going in on their own terms rather than being "committed." In any event, this a time-consuming and emotionally taxing experience.

Handling emergency situations is also aided by knowledge of local resources. For example, your community may have a crisis line that you can call for a full listing of services, such as adult protection, legal council for the elderly, and meals on wheels. Case management is often a necessary part of psychotherapy with older adults, especially those who have no family, are poor, or have significant health problems.

ELDER ABUSE AND NEGLECT

In the course of your first session of psychotherapy with a senior, you may come to suspect that your client is being abused or neglected. Abuse comes in several forms. We automatically think of physical abuse, but there are other forms: psychological abuse (such as intimidation and threats), financial exploitation, civil-rights abuses (such as restricting communication with others), and destruction of personal property. Neglect can also take the form of inadequate nutrition, neglect of medical care, and unsanitary living conditions.

Some older adults are reluctant to share instances of abuse or neglect for fear that the revelation will result in being left without support—or aggravating the abusive behavior. Reading between the lines in a first session may be necessary. For example, recall the eighty-four-year-old woman whose driving was worrisome; she told me that her son "takes care of all my matters." That's probably a benign statement, but it is worthwhile to ask such a person, "What sorts of things does he take care of?" and "Does he take care of your money?" or perhaps "Do you get a say-so in what goes on?"

The suspicion of neglect or abuse is raised when I learn that a primary caregiver is a substance abuser. I remember all too well a case I supervised in which an older divorced woman was living in her rural home. Her only son lived in a mobile home on the same piece of property, free of rent and utilities costs. Our client also provided essentially round-the-clock care for her granddaughter. The child was in her son's full custody. He was a heavy alcohol and drug abuser. He drifted from job to job and behaved irresponsibly; he had repeatedly taken his mother's car without notifying her. Worse, he had left it out of gas on the side of the road on several occasions and wrecked it once. We learned about these problems with her son in the first session, and at that time we simply logged the information. I might add that this client was fully competent in terms of cognitive functioning, though her feelings of fear, anxiety, and anger were quite intense.

Over the course of the next few sessions, we learned that the son was also controlling her finances, pawning her personal belongings, and threatening personal harm. We were concerned about the welfare of the granddaughter as well, but it seemed that our client was doing a good job of surrogate parenting, given the hand she was dealt.

We first tried to empower our client to be more assertive with her son, but this was not successful. She feared him, particularly when he was drunk (which was most of the time), and she was afraid of what might happen to her granddaughter if he got mad and left.

We volunteered to be the bad guys by turning in a report to Adult Protective Services or the police department. She did not like this idea, and in fact we began to believe our focus on this issue was beginning to undermine the therapeutic alliance. To our surprise, she came into the next session requesting that we file a report. Her son had threatened to harm her when she refused to give up her car the previous morning. She was preparing to take her granddaughter to kindergarten when he commandeered the car, leaving our client to call a neighbor for transportation. She had had enough. My supervisee and her client called protective services about the problems she was experiencing. The act of doing something forceful and decisive about her situation represented a liberation of sorts. She became more willing to take a stand with her son.

HELPING ELDERS HANDLE CRISES

The first session with an older client can result in expression of strong emotions and unpleasant realizations. For example, a depressed person may experience profound sadness heretofore untapped, or through beginning to explore a topic may realize that he is indeed not satisfied with the life he has lived. For many seniors, the dialogue that takes place in a therapy session is unlike any interaction they have experienced. My point is that some clients may leave the session feeling overwhelmed and in a mild crisis. Alternatively, they may be in the midst of a crisis when they visit you. What can you do to help?

Here's an example from my work. I saw a sixty-year-old Latino woman while working in Arizona at a rural primary care facility that provided low-cost services. This woman was referred to me by the physician at the clinic because she was having trouble getting over the unexpected death of her husband. In our first meeting, I learned that she spent much of her day crying at home. She slept very little and could not get her husband off her mind. These symptoms had been occurring for about eight months. Physically she looked, shall I say, awful: big black circles under her eyes, disheveled, and gaunt. I surmised during our interview that she was probably below average in intelligence and had almost no problem-focused coping skills. She just felt overwhelmed and did not know what to do.

I knew that I needed to come up with something fast to help her cope. She was unwilling to take benzodiazepines for short-term relief, nor was she willing to take an antidepressant for longer-term benefit. She did have a strong social support network, mainly several adult children who lived nearby, although they too were experiencing protracted grieving. I also learned that her home was practically a shrine to her husband, with pictures and mementos throughout the house. This gave me an idea. I asked her if it would be possible to move the pictures and bric-a-brac to one room in the house.

"If you do this," I said, "I think you'll be better able to control your sad feelings because you won't be reminded of your loss so much."

"But that would be wrong, I'd be forgetting my husband's memory."

"Two things come to mind. One, do you think your husband would want you to be feeling this sad and upset?"

"No he wouldn't. I never thought of it that way."

"To make sure you don't forget your husband's memory, how about if you set aside a half-hour or hour where you go to the room and grieve? My idea is that you'll have some control over things and you'll still be honoring your husband's memory."

"I think a half-hour is enough, don't you?"

"Yeah, I think so," I said.

At our next meeting, she told me that these techniques had decreased the amount of time she spent in crying and being upset. Ultimately, she decided to keep the pictures and items in the room as a special place for her (and her husband).

Other less technical means can be used to help your older client make it through a rough time. Good old reassurance can go a long way. For example, to depressed older adults I have on more than a few occasions said something to this effect: "I know things seem pretty bad now, but I have worked with other people who were in your shoes. Most of them got considerably better over time, and I have a lot of reasons to believe the same will happen for you. What's more, though it may not seem like it, you've been coping with your feelings for the past three months; I think you'll be able to do so for the next few weeks and even beyond. You're pretty tough." I realize most clients don't fully believe this, but it does seem to provide some reassurance.

It is also wise to remind clients in crisis that it is important that they take care of themselves. Getting enough sleep, making sure they have enough to eat, easing up on alcohol, and taking prescription medication only as directed are all good things for a therapist to remind clients about, and to check on them regularly. Being able to say that you have worked with older adults in crisis also lends credibility to your statements.

———————

Crises arise when we work with people in distress. Some situations are relatively unique to seniors and raise questions about competence (to manage self-care, to operate a motor vehicle), as well as about elder abuse and neglect. Other crises are shared across the life span (suicidal ideation). In these situations, it is certainly helpful to know of local resources (hospitals, protective services) and to have colleagues with whom you can consult and get second opinions. Fortunately, most crisis situations are resolved successfully; once this occurs, you are ready to move ahead in treatment. Chapter Seven addresses the question of what's next.

Notes

1. Gatz, M. "Variations on Depression in Later Life." Paper presented at the annual meeting of the American Psychological Association, Chicago, Aug. 1997.

2. Scogin, F., Rohen, N., and Bailey, E. "Geriatric Depression Scale." In M. Maruish (ed.), *Applications of Psychological Testing in Primary Care Settings*. Hillsdale, N.J.: Erlbaum, forthcoming.

7

What's Next?

The first session with a senior is most important, but often not the only one that you have. Let's talk about what comes next as far as treatment planning is concerned. I work from the assumption that the first session permits you to gather a diagnostic impression and build an alliance with your older client. The components of treatment planning that I cover are treatment selection and decisions about referrals.

Let me say from the outset that my orientation to treatment is eclectic, as I mentioned in Chapter Five. Specifically, I find myself most comfortable with what is called technical eclecticism,[1] or the effort to systematically use empirically supported therapies or techniques to optimize success. I believe this stance serves older clients well because they present with problems ranging from basic behavioral (incontinence) to existential (facing death). My allegiance is to my client, not to a brand-name therapy.

CHOOSING TREATMENTS

Older clients often present with complicated problems that demand interdisciplinary treatment. For example, it is not uncommon to coordinate psychological treatment with providers of primary care medicine, medical specialists, neuropsychologists, attorneys, and so forth. Although I recognize the necessity of interconnecting these services, I want to talk about psychosocial treatment independent of the other services.

I consider it fortunate that we now have choices when it comes to psychotherapy for older adults. It was not too long ago that some writers questioned the efficacy of psychosocial treatments for seniors. We now have solid evidence that a variety of treatments work with older adults. Indeed, seniors seem to achieve the same degree of benefit from psychotherapy as do younger adult groups.[2] Therapeutic nihilism concerning older adults is not warranted.

Treatment planning should involve as much collaboration between client and therapist as possible. As a group, older adults may not be sophisticated as to the range of possible goals in treatment. For example, I can remember several older clients who had never considered the possibility that their sleep problems might be addressed in psychotherapy. Part of treatment planning with an older client is, then, educational. The collaborative part comes in determining which issues are most salient or pressing, and what types of treatment might be most attractive to a client. These deliberations are of course aided by the alliance formed in the first session. As I have mentioned previously, developing short-term and longer-term goals with your client is in itself an aid to alliance building. Hope, reassurance, expectancy, and trust are enhanced by developing a therapeutic plan.

A PSYCHOTHERAPY MODEL

It is useful to have a model of psychotherapy, even if one operates within an eclectic orientation. Bob Knight has developed one specifically for older adults: the maturity–specific-challenge model.[3] The major elements of the model are presented in Table 7.1.

As you can see, many of the topics covered in earlier sections of this book are included in Knight's model. On the one hand, it makes clear that seniors enter psychotherapy with certain strengths (for example, greater maturity in areas such as the ability to engage

Table 7.1. The Maturity–Specific-Challenge Model

Element of Maturity	Specific Challenge	Cohort Effect	Context
Cognitive complexity	Chronic illnesses	Cognitive abilities	Age-segregated communities
Postformal reasoning	Disabilities	Education	Aging services agencies
Emotional complexity	Preparation for dying	Word usage	Senior recreation sites
Androgyny	Grieving for loved ones	Values	Medical settings
Expertise		Normative life paths	Long-term care
Areas of competency Multiple family experiences Accumulated inter-personal skills		Social historical life experience	Age-based law and regulations

Source: Knight, B. G. "Overview of Psychotherapy with the Elderly: The Contextual, Cohort-Based, Maturity-Specific-Challenge Model." In S. H. Zarit and B. G. Knight (eds.), *A Guide to Psychotherapy and Aging.* Copyright © 1996 by the American Psychological Association. Reprinted with permission.

in complex reasoning about moral dilemmas, and greater expertise thanks to having had more experience with life circumstances). In short, I term this "wisdom."

On the other hand, older adults do, to a greater extent than young people, face some specific challenges. These include chronic illnesses, disabilities, and grieving. Likewise, they were socialized during a different time period. Finally, the social context in which seniors live requires understanding; it includes specific environments (for instance, long-term care) and specific rules (Social Security regulations, Medicare regulations, guardianship laws, and so on).

Considering these elements as you begin working with a senior provides a useful heuristic. The maturity–specific-challenge model can be integrated with particular psychotherapies that have received empirical validation.

EMPIRICALLY SUPPORTED TREATMENTS

Another aid to treatment planning is the effort to determine which treatments actually work for seniors. A set of criteria were applied to the gerontological literature to determine which treatments are "empirically supported."[4] A number of disorders and problems were evaluated, including behavior problems among dementia patients, depression, sleep disorders, and memory problems. What resulted was a list of treatments having empirical support. This does not mean that these are the only treatment modalities that are effective; it does mean that sufficient research has been conducted on these treatments to meet objective criteria for effectiveness.

Empirically Supported Depression Treatment

Let's take depression as an example. Three therapy approaches have passed muster: cognitive, behavioral, and brief psychodynamic therapies. All three have supporting treatment manuals[5] that can inform your work with a depressed senior. I have found it extremely helpful to have some ideas about how to structure the treatment, the therapist's stance, and a sequence to follow. Further, some of these guides are written specifically for older adult clients and take into account many of the issues covered in this book. Still, most older adult cases you treat do not present with an issue so discrete that some technical eclecticism is not called for. For example, many depressed older adult clients present with both maladaptive information processing styles that warrant cognitive therapy techniques and, concurrently, dysfunctional interpersonal relationships that suggest an interpersonal or psychoanalytically oriented psychotherapy stance. I mention this because some people view psychotherapy manuals as rigid, didactic, and mechanistic, and thus eschew them. My perspective is instead that they are guides that provide ideas about how to use a particular theoretically driven and empirically supported treatment.

Empirically Supported Reminiscence Therapy

Interestingly, structured life review or reminiscence therapy was also viewed as a potentially efficacious treatment for depressive symptoms. As you may recall, this is a treatment approach grounded in Erikson's life-span developmental work. To my knowledge, it is a treatment used exclusively with seniors. Sessions are organized around such themes as growing up, World War II, being a parent, and having grandchildren. Sharing memories about happy times can be an aid to morale and well-being, and the social activity can diminish feelings of isolation and loneliness. Reminiscence therapy is usually offered in groups but can be used as individual therapy.

Our research group is presently conducting reminiscence groups at several local nursing homes. These groups are offered to mildly demented residents with the goal of improving quality of life, decreasing dysphoric affect, and increasing social activities. The groups are organized around successive themes, as mentioned above. In listening to the tapes of these groups, I have been impressed with how animated and interactive some of the otherwise placid participants become when discussing the topics. For example, one of them is pets. Almost everyone has a pleasant memory of a pet and enjoys sharing favorite memories about the animal. Many of the participants were raised in rural environments, and recollecting a favorite farm cat or dog seems particularly enjoyable.

Behavior Therapy for Dementia

Another approach to treatment that receives endorsement may be of interest to you: behavioral interventions for persons with dementia. These interventions may be useful if you are providing treatment to a caregiver. Behavioral programs have been developed to address such problems as aggression, wandering, and incontinence. Self-care activities have also been the target of interventions, including bathing, walking, and eating.

Techniques used include learning principles such as reinforcement and extinction, stimulus control, and time out. For example, differential reinforcement is a relatively simple procedure in which a reward (usually staff attention) is given to the patient if a certain behavior (say, physical aggression) has not occurred in a specific time interval. An aggressive cycle may be begun by staff requests (such as getting dressed) and then maintained by staff attention.[6] Differential reinforcement can begin to break this cycle.

Memory Training

Another class of interventions that deserve some discussion are those concerned with memory and cognitive training. On several occasions in this book, I have mentioned that training to help seniors improve memory performance is a useful adjunct for many of them. A colleague and I wrote a book on this topic several years ago,[7] in which we present information on how to use mnemonic techniques to better recall names and faces, lists, and numbers. We also discuss ways to help older adults make their environments more memory-friendly by using physical reminders and cues. For example, I remember an older male European American client who was concerned about his difficulty in remembering names. This was important to him because he did considerable volunteer work and was introduced to many people. We talked about the mnemonic technique of novel interacting images. In brief, it involves making an image out a name ("Brodsky" might be an image of a very wide pair of skis). Then you ask the client to choose a characteristic part of the person (perhaps his bald head) and make the feature and image interact in some vivid or memorable way. This might be an image of someone sliding down the person's slick dome on a set of broad skis. My client really liked this "game," as he called it. We also discussed how to handle his memory lapses with humor, that is, something along the lines of "I'm old and can't remember anything anymore. What did you say your name was?"

Meta-analytic reviews suggest that memory training programs result in improved memory performance and better perceptions of memory functioning.[8]

REFERRALS

Referral decisions are often made following a first session. For example, among many questions that may arise are these:

- Should I refer my client for adjunctive pharmacotherapy?

- Should a referral be made to a social service agency to meet a client need such as transportation or home health care?

- Should I refer this case for psychotherapy by a geriatric mental health specialist?

Pharmacotherapy

I make a decision to refer an older client for pharmacotherapy based on the severity of the presenting disorder and my client's willingness to take medication. Severely depressed and anxious clients often need a rather quick boost to their biochemistry to be able to engage fully in psychotherapy. However, some seniors with whom I have worked adamantly refuse pharmacotherapy, even in the case of a severe major depressive episode. In some cases, the refusal is based on faulty information—for example, that antidepressants are addictive. Other older clients are just philosophically opposed to taking medication, a stance that I can respect.

One client whom I saw, a seventy-year-old Hispanic man, was opposed to taking an antidepressant. Interestingly, he was taking medication for diabetes but saw the antidepressant in very different terms. To him, it showed personal weakness and an admission that he couldn't handle things. I worked on drawing the parallel between medication for depression and medication for diabetes. I tried not to push, but I really thought it would be good for him. The physician at the rural health clinic was in favor of pharmacotherapy as well. Eventually (over several sessions), we persuaded him to start medication, and he had a good response. I'm glad we stuck with it.

Another factor to consider is if your client can be treated pharmacologically by the primary care physician, or if referral to a psychiatrist is more apt. My default is to contact the primary care doctor and let the physician determine (with my input, if desired) whether the case warrants a specialist.

Social Service

Making decisions about hooking up a client or family with a social service agency is not that hard. If the need exists, I do not hesitate to make a call. The client must of course agree and be willing to cooperate with the service provider. Some clients seem a bit ashamed and disheartened by having to rely on "outsiders," but I have found that some reassurance and gentle cognitive therapy work to reduce these feelings.

For example, at the end of an initial session with an older African American male client, I became quite concerned that he was not eating well. This was not due to depression but to his limited culinary skills and some difficulty with dexterity.

"Since you're having some trouble cooking," I said, "how would it be for us to get in contact with the meals-on-wheels people? They are the folks who bring meals to you on a regular basis."

"Well . . . I don't much care for taking handouts like that. I'd rather take care of myself."

"I can understand that; you've been an independent and productive person all your life. So it's hard to think about getting help like this. But I don't see this as a sign of weakness; I see it as a way to help you maintain your independence. If you don't eat right, you'll get sick and maybe get moved out of your home. So, I see accepting this service as a way to keep your independence. Besides, you never liked to cook anyway!"

He chuckled and nodded his head as I went on.

"I'll bet you wouldn't judge harshly someone who was receiving meals-on-wheels who was in a situation like yours."

"No, not if they really needed it."

"I don't think you deserve your own harsh judgment."

He thought about for a week and decided to try it. It turned out to be, in his words, "One of the best things I have ever done for myself."

Geriatric Mental Health Specialist

One referral question I have not covered is under what conditions you should consider referring a client to a geriatric mental health specialist (assuming you are not one). Phenomenologically, I advise considering it whenever you have the feeling that you're getting in over your head. As the complexity of the case increases, the need for specialty training increases. For example, treatment of a sixty-five-year-old, community-dwelling, healthy person with generalized anxiety disorder probably does not call for a specialist. On the other hand, if you are concluding a first session with a sixty-five-year-old who is being treated for congestive heart failure, has had several minor strokes, is taking several medications, has a history of recurrent major depression, and is being cared for by a controlling son-in-law, maybe the thought of consultation or referral should cross your mind.

How do you know someone is a specialist? Word of mouth goes a long way, no doubt. More formal credentialing is in progress, at least as far as psychology is concerned. The American Psychological Association has recently approved a proficiency designation in clinical geropsychology, much like specialties in neuropsychology and substance abuse. This designation recognizes the need for specialized training and helps both professionals and consumers identify those with particular expertise. I expect that other disciplines such as social work, psychiatry, and nursing will also develop similar designations within their mental health concentration areas, if they have not already done so.

Other Specialized Services

You may have some other services in your community that are worth consideration. For example, specialized geropsychiatry inpatient facilities are available at some hospitals. Day care programs for seniors with dementia are a valuable resource for family caregivers. In our community, these programs are run as not-for-profit services and organized through church congregations. Thus, the cost is reasonable.

Assisted-living care facilities, retirement living centers, and nursing homes are other resources that a person working with older adults should know about. In our community there is also a legal center that delivers low-cost services for seniors; I have referred several clients to this service who wished to prepare an advanced directive (such as a do-not-resuscitate order) or wanted to amend their wills.

Respite facilities are another resource you will be asked about if you work with family caregivers. Respite allows caregivers to have a break from caring for a family member for short periods.

This list is obviously not exhaustive but gives you an idea about services that enhance your work with seniors and their families.

The availability of various effective treatments for seniors puts treatment planning on sound ground. Yet the diversity of client problems and characteristics makes flexibility a crucial attribute of a good therapist. Part of this flexibility is knowing when to make a referral for a medication consultation and when to make a referral to a mental health specialist who is trained to work with seniors. Regardless of whether or not you are a specialist, knowledge of other services such as respite, meals on wheels, and legal assistance is a plus.

In the final chapter, I present a couple of cases with which I hope to demonstrate some of the ideas presented in this and the preceding chapters.

Notes

1. Lazarus, A. A., Beutler, L. E., and Norcross, J. C. "The Future of Technical Eclecticism." *Psychotherapy*, 1992, *29*, 11–20.

2. Scogin, F., and McElreath, L. "Efficacy of Psychosocial Treatments for Geriatric Depression: A Quantitative Review." *Journal of Consulting and Clinical Psychology*, 1994, *62*, 69–74.

3. Knight, B. G. "Overview of Psychotherapy with the Elderly: The Contextual, Cohort-Based, Maturity–Specific-Challenge Model." In S. H. Zarit and B. G. Knight (eds.), *A Guide to Psychotherapy and Aging*. Washington, D.C.: American Psychological Association, 1996.

4. Gatz, M., and others. "Empirically Validated Treatments for Older Adults." *Journal of Mental Health and Aging*. (forthcoming).

5. Beck, A. T., Rush, J., Shaw, B., and Emery, G. *Cognitive Therapy of Depression*. New York: Guilford Press, 1979; Gallagher, D., and Thompson, L. W. *Depression in the Elderly: A Behavioral Treatment, Manual*. Los Angeles: University of Southern California Press, 1981; Mann, J. *Time-Limited Therapy*. Cambridge, Mass.: Harvard University Press, 1973.

6. Burgio, L. D., Cotter, E. M., and Stevens, A. B. "Treatment in Residential Settings." In M. Hersen and V. B. Van Hasselt (eds.), *Psychological Treatment of Older Adults*. New York: Plenum, 1996.

7. Scogin, F., and Prohaska, M. *Aiding Older Adults with Memory Complaints*. Sarasota, Fla.: Professional Resource Exchange, 1993.

8. Verhaeghen, P., Marcoen, A., and Goossens, L. "Improving Memory Performance in the Aged Through Mnemonic Training: A Meta-Analytic Study." *Psychology and Aging*, 1992, *7*, 242–251; Floyd, M., and Scogin, F. "Effects of Memory Training on the Subjective Memory Functioning and Mental Health of Older Adults: A Meta-Analysis." *Psychology and Aging*, 1997, *12*, 150–161.

8

Case Studies

This chapter consists of two case studies with which I demonstrate the first-session strategies overviewed in this book. These cases are composites of various cases I have seen or supervised; they were created to illustrate aspects of work with older clients.

THE CASE OF M.

M. is a sixty-seven-year-old female who was referred to me by a private practice psychiatrist who works in a nearby town. A retired bookkeeper, M. was referred to the psychiatrist by her cardiac surgeon because she had become extremely depressed following open-heart surgery.

M.'s psychiatrist contacted me to ask if I would be willing to see her for psychotherapy. The psychiatrist informed me that M. had been on a selective serotonin re-uptake inhibitor (SSRI) for approximately one year, and that she had experienced a significant, but not total, reduction in depressive symptoms. The referral for psychotherapy was to treat these remaining symptoms and, more important, address an issue that was significantly affecting her quality of life: pessimism. Her psychiatrist knew that I specialized in cognitive-behavior therapy for depressed seniors and thought I might be able to help her with these problems. We agreed that continued pharmacotherapy was warranted and that we would stay in touch as to

M.'s progress, should she decide she wanted to try psychotherapy. The psychiatrist told me that M. had agreed to psychotherapy when he brought it up.

I contacted M. to set up our initial session. I was immediately struck by her mental acuity. She understood the purpose of my call and was quick to locate her schedule book so that we could work out a time. She wrote down the directions to my office and thought far enough ahead to ask about parking difficulties. She was soft-spoken, but more distinctive was her air of resignation. For example, in response to my parting comment that "I look forward to seeing you," she responded, "I look forward to seeing you, but I don't think I can shake this gloomy attitude I have." *Meta-pessimism,* I thought to myself, *she's pessimistic about pessimism.*

M. was on time to her appointment. As I introduced myself, I thought, *I bet she is going to be interesting.* She was wearing high-top sneakers, blue jeans, and handmade jewelry. She wore no makeup, and her hair was cut in a style more often seen in younger women. I thought, *She may be sixty-seven in chronological years, but she is much younger in social years.* This impression would be borne out by information I gathered during our first session.

I began by saying, "What I'd like for us to do today is talk about your reasons for coming for treatment and what you'd like to get out of it. I'll also try to give you some ideas on how treatment might proceed based on what we learn." Note that I presented three discrete bits of information in this paragraph. If there had been reason to believe that M. had some degree of cognitive impairment, I would have simplified.

I followed this brief agenda overview with a statement concerning the limits of confidentiality. M. seemed attentive but not particularly moved by these preliminary proceedings. She nodded her head to indicate understanding of what I was saying but had no questions and did not raise her eyebrows, as I have seen some clients do when I tell them under what conditions I might break confidentiality.

I then said to her, "I've talked to your psychiatrist about you. but I'd like to hear in your own words your reasons for coming in today." She said, "I feel like I'm losing control because my health keeps getting worse and worse and I see no hope that things are going to get any better."

I asked her about her health problems and learned that in addition to her cardiovascular problems she had suffered from diabetes for more than twenty years. This created a number of complications, including amputation of her big toe. Missing a big toe, she had trouble with balance and walking, so much so that she had fallen several times. On one fall, she fractured her leg. She was rightfully concerned that she might break her hip or hit her head the next time she fell. She refused to use a cane or walker because that would be incompatible with her self-image of an active and independent person. "I'm not a blue-haired old lady," she said.

M. also felt out of control because she had recently been forced to move out of her home of forty years. Her declining health and forced relocation were tremendous losses and created a sense of hopelessness that touched me emotionally.

After we had discussed these issues, I knew there would be no need for memory and cognitive testing. M. showed good memory for recent events and had no problems in keeping up with the flow of our conversation. At one point in the session, I did ask her if she had any problems with memory, and she stated, "My memory is OK, but I definitely don't remember things as well as I did when I was working." When I asked for specific examples, she said she had to rely on notes to remember things now, whereas before she didn't need that kind of help. *We should all be so lucky*, I thought to myself! Nonetheless, I made a note to discuss compensatory memory strategies with her at a later date.

I also asked her about her history, to gain an appreciation of context: "Tell me a little about your family, your work, your children if you have any, and so forth." M. had been a widow for about twenty-five years and had raised four children as a single parent. *Whew*, I thought to myself, *I'm raising two with a spouse and it's quite a job.* She had two years of college credits but was forced to give up part-time higher education when her husband died. For most of her employed years, she worked as a bookkeeper for a small business and as a clerk for a judge. She was proud of herself for raising her children but expressed some regret that they had not had a father. She wondered if she made the right decision not to remarry.

Her children were living various distances away, so asking them to get involved, at least physically, was not an option. M. indicated that she loved all her children but that she worried about two of them. Both had divorced, and she was concerned about their well-being and that of her three grandchildren.

As we talked, I realized she was very intelligent, probably in the superior range on conventional IQ tests. I could also tell that she was open to new experience and was inquisitive. For example, she told me she surfed the Internet and listened to contemporary music. These tendencies suggested to me that psychotherapy could be conducted at a more abstract level if need be and that she would probably be amenable to trying out new things that I might ask of her.

As our session unfolded, a picture of this older client emerged: a cognitively intact, moderately depressed woman who was experiencing significant health-related problems and a striking sense of hopelessness and pessimism. The latter were, of course, the reasons for her referral to me.

Toward the middle of the session, I began to assess M.'s current level of depressive symptomatology. I went down a list of the DSM-IV criteria, asking for duration and intensity of symptoms. She reported no problems with her appetite; in fact, she had scarcely any somatic indicants of depression. More psychological markers of depression were present. For example, when I asked her, "Have you noticed you've lost interest in things you used to do?" she answered: "I haven't lost interest in them altogether, but I don't seem to have the motivation to do things I used to. I know it would probably be better for me." I also asked, "Do you find yourself feeling guilty about things?" to which she responded: "Yes, a lot. I'm guilty that I've let friends down who rely on me, and I'm guilty that I've begun to be a burden for my children. I can't seem to shake thoughts like that. There are also a lot of things I wanted to do when I retired, and now it doesn't look like I'll get to."

Finally, I asked about suicide.

"Do you sometimes have thoughts that life isn't worth living?"

"Almost daily."

"When you have these thoughts what are you thinking?"

"I think that because things are not going to get better—my health, you know—I'd save myself some suffering if I ended my life now. Plus, I don't enjoy things like I used, and I feel like I don't have control of what's happening to me. I'm not used to feeling that way, at least not this much."

"That sounds tough, particularly since you're not used to feeling this way. When you have thoughts about hurting yourself, do you think about ways you might do it?"

"Yes, I think about taking some pills, probably sleeping medication, and drinking some wine and going to sleep. What keeps me from doing it is I don't have the pills and I'm not sure I'd kill myself. I'd want it to be over with for my sake and my family's sake."

"So it sounds like you have an idea about how to commit suicide, but you don't have the means to do so and you're not sure you'd pull it off correctly."

"That's right, but I think it is only a matter of time."

This information on suicide, of course, concerned me. I asked her if she had told her psychiatrist about this, and she said she had. This led to a discussion of her discontent with her current psychiatrist and a desire to get back to her first one. She had changed psychiatrists when the first moved about thirty miles away. The new one, who had referred her to me, was rather young (about thirty-five), had been in the military, and was "used to telling people what to do." M. said that didn't work too well with her. (I made a mental note to go easy on the directive techniques.) We discussed the possibility of her returning to the first psychiatrist, and I offered to help her with this potentially awkward situation. I felt a sense of trust and alliance develop from that gesture, as if I had communicated to her that I was on her side, not a shill for my referral source.

Nonetheless, the immediate issue of suicide risk remained. I judged her not to be an imminent risk but got an agreement that she would call me or one of the two psychiatrists should her feelings of hopelessness intensify. I also obtained her written permission to discuss the matter with psychiatrist number two.

At this point, we were nearing the end of our first session. I let her know that it was time to talk about where we might go from there. I had reached a preliminary primary diagnosis of major depression in partial remission with marked features of hopelessness and pessimism. My conceptualization of M. was quite similar to that of psychiatrist number two. I decided to give her a brief overview of cognitive-behavior therapy for depression and how the treatment might unfold. She seemed to be receptive to the idea of meeting twice a week for a few weeks and then shifting to once a week. She was particularly receptive to the idea of working on her thinking patterns: "My thinking is so negative. I'd like to be more optimistic, but my situation is hopeless." Being a believer in therapeutic homework and bibliotherapy, I mentioned to her that I had read a book that helped me be more optimistic[1] and asked if she would like to look at it. Being open to experience, she agreed. I felt as if her acceptance of the book was both an indicant of a beginning alliance and a sign that her pessimism was not insurmountable.

Epilogue

M. represents a case in which cognitive impairment is not an issue and as such the flow of communication is much like that with a younger client. I demonstrated respect for M. by initially calling her "Mrs.," although she quickly told me to call her M. I also demonstrated respect by taking her complaints about her psychiatrist seriously and not treating them as pessimistic mutterings from a depressed old lady. I also walked her to and from her car—a little thing that meant a lot, I could tell.

M. did in fact engage in psychotherapy. She made strides in reducing her dysfunctional thinking, but she still has ups and downs. We now meet about once a month for maintenance sessions, and she continues her pharmacotherapy. She got back with psychiatrist number one and is pleased with their relationship. During a recent session, she said to me, "You know more about me than any one else ever has." *What a privilege*, I thought.

THE CASE OF MRS. S.

Mrs. S. is a seventy-four-year-old, African American female referred to me by a friend of hers. Mr. S. called me to set up the appointment, indicating that his wife seemed distraught and was having memory troubles. I scheduled a first session and asked Mr. S. to attend.

Knowing that cognition would probably be an issue, I had the MMSE handy. When the couple arrived for the appointment, it was apparent that Mr. S.'s description was accurate; she did indeed looked distraught. Throughout the session, she wrung her hands, cried often, and repeatedly stated, "I just don't know what to do." Her husband was somber, almost in a state of grieving, and he too did not know what to do. She appeared to be a healthy woman; she reported no chronic health problems. She did indicate a bout of postmenopausal depression that was successfully treated by an antidepressant, and hypothyroidism that was being treated by a thyroid medication.

As I began the session, I was curious about how Mr. and Mrs. S. would interact. He did not jump in to answer questions for her but did provide cues when she seemed to have trouble answering. For example, I asked her what some of her favorite activities were, and he reminded her about her gardening. She was then able to describe in some detail the flowers and vegetables she tended. I noticed that she demonstrated longer-than-expected response latency when I spoke to her. These observations suggested to me that a brief cognitive screening would be in order.

The need for such a screening was confirmed when I asked Mr. S. about his concerns. He was a successful businessman, and she had handled the office duties for the couple's various business concerns over the course of their marriage of almost fifty years. He stated that he had been increasingly concerned about her memory lapses and concentration difficulties. Although she had at one time handled appointments, bookkeeping, and all tax duties, she was now having difficulty remembering even simple things like when to pay bills and the names of regular vendors. He had noticed her having trouble with the taxes approximately four months earlier. He also noticed that her moods were increasingly unpredictable, that she had lost weight, and that her interest in most of the couple's social activities was waning.

He also reported that she had recently begun showing concern about unknown "others" who were "judging" her. When I asked her if these descriptions seemed about right, she nodded and said, "Yes, I just don't know what to do." This was a tough interview to conduct because Mrs. S. seemed inconsolable and her husband seemed overwhelmed by the enormity of what had transpired over the past several months. He often looked downward, slowly shook his head, and tears welled in his eyes.

I asked them if they had sought any help for their problems before seeing me. She had seen a psychiatrist at the urging of her husband and two sons. According to Mr. S., his wife had been diagnosed with bipolar disorder and started on lithium carbonate and an anticonvulsive medication. They were not clear why she had been diagnosed with bipolar disorder. Soon after starting this regimen, she began to have trouble sleeping, became more anxious and suspicious, and was admitted to an inpatient psychiatric facility five days later. She saw me approximately one month after her hospitalization.

She received a neurological examination during her brief hospitalization. Her husband said the neurologist told them that the examination revealed memory problems, and a CT scan showed that cortical atrophy was present. The CT also suggested findings consistent with multiple small strokes. The psychiatrist added an SSRI antidepressant to her medications and discharged her with the recommendation that her husband begin to look into nursing care for her.

Mr. and Mrs. S. were uncertain and somewhat upset about what had transpired in her treatment. They were seeking a second opinion when they contacted me. I think they also hoped that someone would be able to give them a less discouraging prognosis.

"It seems," I said about halfway through the session, "your husband and your doctor have some concerns about memory. I understand you're worried also. Would it be OK if I asked you some questions and had you do a few things that would help me get a feel for this?" She had no problem with the request, so I did a Mini-Mental.

It confirmed that she did show working-memory deficits, but it did not reveal deficits that would suggest dementia. Her total score was 26. I thought she would need a more thorough neuropsychological examination and made a mental note to refer them to one of my colleagues who is a specialist in geriatric neuropsychology.

I asked Mrs. S. how she thought she had done on the MMSE; she said, "Not very well." It seemed very difficult for her to provide much elaboration or content on any particular subject before she would begin to wring her hands and lament her plight. However, when I asked her about her life she seemed to relax a bit. This well-rehearsed information was familiar terrain for her. She reported an unremarkable childhood and graduation from the state university. She trained as a teacher and planned to return to her hometown upon graduation. She met Mr. S. while at the university, and they married soon thereafter. She handled the books for him and raised the couple's two sons. As we talked, I noticed that she responded well to attempts at humor. This seemed to reduce her level of distress, at least temporarily.

As our first session neared an end, I realized I had more questions than answers about her case. I first tried to summarize to the couple what I had learned, to assure us all that I had the facts rights: "Here's what I've heard you say today. If I get off base, correct me, OK? These problems that you've been having started about four months ago. You noticed that your wife was having trouble with office tasks that normally were not much of a problem for her. Mrs. S., it sounds like you noticed these changes in your memory and concentration too. This was upsetting, of course, to both of you. Since you didn't know what was going on, you did the right thing and sought the services of a specialist, a psychiatrist. He started you on a medication to treat your symptoms and had you stay in the hospital a few days to get things stabilized. You didn't leave there with good news, as I understand it. Is that about right?"

As I considered how to end the session, I knew that something wasn't right in this picture. A first episode of bipolar affective disorder in later life is rare; I knew this based on information from epidemiological literature. I also knew that most dementing illnesses, particularly Alzheimer's disease, have a much slower and insidious onset, whereas in Mrs. S.'s case the change in her cognitive functioning had been rather abrupt. There were, however, the results of the CT scan that raised the possibility of dementia. It was also a bit atypical to see someone wringing her hands and presenting with such labile emotions. My face must have looked like a big question mark.

"I'm not really sure what is going on," I told them, "except I know for sure that you're upset. I'd like us to meet again in a few days to talk about how you might cope with this situation better. In the meantime, I'd like to get permission to talk to your doctor and your psychiatrist. Maybe if we all put our heads together we can come up with a plan to help you. I'd also like to get in touch with someone who could do a thorough evaluation of your memory. Would you being willing to do this?"

She agreed. I asked them if they had any questions for me. He did.

"Do you think she has Alzheimer's disease?"

"That may be the case, but I really can't say for sure. Has anyone told you she has Alzheimer's?"

"No, but it seems like it's been implied. I was told to start looking for a place to care for her. That sounds pretty bad."

In this case, I did not do an orientation to a particular treatment because I wasn't sure what treatment would be appropriate. I closed the session by scheduling a second one. As I watched them depart, I felt heavyhearted by the anguish they were experiencing.

Epilogue

Soon after the session with the couple, I got in touch with their primary care doctor and asked him about her recent medical history. In looking at her chart, he noted that she had begun treatment for hypothyroidism about five months ago. Otherwise, she was in good health. He knew of her treatment by the psychiatrist but not much of the details. He described her as a little flamboyant and perhaps given to exaggeration. I asked him about any signs of cognitive impairment; "Not much," he said, "beyond what I'd expect given her age."

After this consultation, a realization came to me. The onset of the treatment for hypothyroidism closely coincided with the change in her cognitive functioning and emotional well-being. I wondered if her symptoms might have something to do with the thyroid supplement. As I thought more about it, it came to me that her symptoms could be viewed as *hyper*thyroidism. I called her physician again and he returned the call that night at home. We discussed my observation, and he said it might be worth getting an updated lab report.

It turns out that the onset of Mrs. S.'s symptoms and her thyroid treatment were more than coincident. Her doctor informed us that her lab work had been incorrect and that she was not hypothyroid at the time she began the thyroid supplement. Her somewhat dramatic presentation style and increased anxiety and emotional lability had led the psychiatrist to a diagnosis of bipolar disorder.

Mrs. S.'s doctor consulted with her psychiatrist, and the psychiatric medications were discontinued. Over several weeks, her mood and cognitive functioning improved. My role was then to monitor and help them cope with what I would describe, in DSM-IV terms, as acute stress disorder. Acute stress disorder is the reaction to a traumatic event that can precede development of PTSD. I would certainly describe the couple's experience as traumatic.

These cases demonstrate that some knowledge of gerontology can be beneficial in working with seniors. This is particularly true for first sessions, in which a great deal of information must be synthesized to render diagnoses and make plans for treatment. However, a first session is not just a process of collecting information; it is also the beginning of a therapeutic relationship. In these cases, I hope that I have conveyed a sense of respect for my clients, for I believe this is an important aspect of rapport building with seniors.

Finally, being an advocate for your older client is sometimes a necessity, as these cases illustrate. This takes time and may not be billable, but it is part of the job.

Note

1. Seligman, M. E. P. *Learned Optimism: The Skill to Conquer Life's Obstacles, Large and Small.* New York: Random House, 1991.

Afterword

A number of years ago, someone came up with the idea of the YAVIS client. The notion (albeit sarcastic) is that the ideal client should be young, attractive, verbal, intelligent, and . . . something that starts with S that I can never remember. After a few years of clinical work, I concluded that they had it wrong: it should be OAVIS—older, rather than younger.

In truth, research supports none of these client characteristics as related to treatment outcome. My point is that work with older adults is challenging and rewarding. I hope that I have captured both of these aspects in this book on the first session with seniors. The challenges brought by cognitive changes, health issues, and family involvement, and the rewards of seeing a person in despair move toward integrity, are a part of work with older clients.

With the changing demographic landscape, it is highly likely that the psychotherapist of the twenty-first century will work with clients in their sixties, seventies, eighties, and nineties, and even centenarians. Psychosocial treatment has a part to play in improving the quality of life of seniors or (as I have heard it said) "putting life in the living." I encourage you to continue your education in gerontology, as I do, by reading journals and books from the explosion of interest in aging and mental health. More important, see older adult clients, and learn from them.

Good luck!

Further Reading

Carstensen, L. L., Edelstein, B. A., and Dornbrand, L. *The Practical Handbook of Clinical Gerontology*. Thousand Oaks, Calif.: Sage, 1996.

Hartman-Stein, P. E. *Innovative Behavioral Healthcare for Older Adults*. San Francisco: Jossey-Bass, 1998.

Hersen, M., and Van Hasselt, V. B. *Psychological Treatment of Older Adults*. New York: Plenum, 1996.

Nordhus, I. H., VandenBos, G. R., Berg, S., and Fromholt, P. *Clinical Geropsychology*. Washington, D.C.: American Psychological Association, 1998.

Papalia, D. E., Camp, C. J., and Feldman, R. D. *Adult Development and Aging*. New York: McGraw-Hill, 1996.

Zarit, S. H., and Knight, B. G. *A Guide to Psychotherapy and Aging*. Washington, D.C.: American Psychological Association, 1996.

The Author

Forrest Scogin is professor of psychology and director of graduate studies in the Department of Psychology at the University of Alabama in Tuscaloosa. He earned his B.A. degree (1977) in psychology at the University of Tennessee in Knoxville, and both his M.A. (1980) and Ph.D. (1983) in clinical psychology at Washington University in St. Louis. He completed a postdoctoral fellowship (1984) in health psychology and psychotherapy research at the University of Arizona Health Sciences Center in Tucson.

Scogin's research activities have been in clinical geropsychology. He has published on such topics as the treatment of depression and anxiety among seniors, memory training, and the mental health needs of rural older adults. He has received extensive external funding for these research activities.

Scogin is a Fellow of the American Psychological Association Divisions 12 (Clinical) and 20 (Adult Development and Aging). He maintains a private practice that focuses on treating seniors and is a sport psychology consultant to the University of Alabama Athletics Department.

Index

F

Family members: denial of, about cognitive impairment, 69–70; elder abuse and neglect by, 97, 115–117; expectations of, for treatment, 37; as initiators of therapy, 3, 34–37; involving, in first session, 5, 34, 103–104; substance abuse by, 115–116. *See also* Adult children; Spouses

Family therapy, 34

Fatigability, 40, 41

Fatigue, in session, 94–95

Female versus male older adults, 8, 11

Finances, problems with handling, 34, 35, 62, 105

Financial exploitation, 115, 116

First session with older adults: agenda for, 96–103; alliance building in, 73–89; assessment in, 53–67; case studies of, 133–144; in cognitive impairment case study, 139–144; countertransference in, 80–81, 84–89; crisis intervention in, 105–119; in depression case study, 133–139; diagnosis in, 4, 67–71; importance of, 2–3; interviewing strategies for, 91–104; involving family members in, 5, 34, 103–104; overview of, 3–5; planning and preparation for, 76, 91, 96–103; presenting problems in, 40–44; referral sources to, 33–40; therapy orientation in, 99–102; transference in, 80–84; treatment planning after, 121–131; treatment planning at end of, 102–103

Five-factor model of personality, 15–17

Food offerings, 84

Functional age, 13

G

Gaston, L., 73–74, 76, 89

Gender differences, in life expectancy, 8, 11

Generalized anxiety disorder (GAD), 42, 69, 102

Generational differences: learning about, 77–78; in perceptions of mental health, 17–18; in perceptions of treatment, 19–20; in personality, 16–17

Generativity versus stagnation, 26

Geriatric Depression Scale (GDS), 41–42

Geriatric psychiatrists/mental health specialists: as referral sources, 39; referral to, 127, 129–130

Geropsychology: expertise in, 2, 8, 129–130, 144; primer in, 7–29; readings in, 29, 147

Glaucoma, 24

Good son or daughter, therapist as, 82, 84, 85

Great Depression, 16, 77

Grief: helping elders handle, 117–119; over death of adult child, 48; over death of spouse, 47–48; over spouse with Alzheimer's disease, 48; as presenting problem, 47–48. *See also* Bereavement; Death

Group therapy, reminiscence, 125

"Guidelines for the Evaluation of Dementia and Age-Related Cognitive Decline," 62

Guilt feelings, 26, 28, 136–137

H

Health problems: anxiety and, 42–43; depression coexistent with, 40; of older adults, 14–15. *See also* Chronic health conditions; Medical status assessment

Health status, of older adults, 14–15. *See also* Chronic health conditions; Medical status assessment

Hearing impairment, 23, 93

Heterogeneity, 14

Historical events: demonstrating knowledge about, 77–78; as socializing influences, 16–17